12/19 ꜱ   peta

Digital Life Skills for Youth

Digital Life Skills for Youth

A Guide for Parents, Guardians, and Educators

Angela Crocker

Self-Counsel Press
(a division of)
International Self-Counsel Press Ltd.
Canada   USA

Self-Counsel Press acknowledges the financial support of the Government of Canada through the Canada Book Fund (CBF) for our publishing activities. Canada

Printed in Canada.

First edition: 2019

Library and Archives Canada Cataloguing in Publication

Title: Digital life skills for youth : a guide for parents, guardians, and educators / Angela Crocker.

Names: Crocker, Angela, author.

Series: Self-Counsel reference series.

Description: Series statement: Reference series

Identifiers: Canadiana (print) 20190148861 | Canadiana (ebook) 20190148896 | ISBN 9781770403147 (softcover) | ISBN 9781770405042 (EPUB) | ISBN 9781770405059 (Kindle)

Subjects: LCSH: Internet and children. | LCSH: Computers and children. | LCSH: Computer literacy. | LCSH: Internet literacy. | LCSH: Information society.

Classification: LCC QA76.9.C64 C76 2019 | DDC 004—dc23

Self-Counsel Press
(a division of)
International Self-Counsel Press Ltd.

North Vancouver, BC
Canada

Bellingham, WA
USA

Contents

6 Safety Skills

Conclusion

Download Kit

Samples

Notice to Readers

Laws are constantly changing. Every effort is made to keep this publication as current as possible. However, the author, the publisher, and the vendor of this book make no representations or warranties regarding the outcome or the use to which the information in this book is put and are not assuming any liability for any claims, losses, or damages arising out of the use of this book. The reader should not rely on the author or the publisher of this book for any professional advice. Please be sure that you have the most recent edition.

Dedication

For Sean, an emerging digital citizen, who inspires me every day.

Acknowledgments

With special thanks to my husband, Paul. We are different kinds of geek but we are a dynamic duo when it comes to digital parenting.

Deep appreciation to Dear Ol' Dad, Brian, who introduced my brother and me to computers at an early age. And to my treasured brother, Michael, with whom I argued over the controls of our TI99/4A, Commodore 64, and other home computers.

Thanks also to the awesome youth who call me Auntie Angela. Their questions and behaviors around digital things inspired me to make this book the best it could be. I'm talking about you: Owen, Alana, Pippa, Alexander, Caroline, Grace, Ella, Elizabeth, Mitch, Kaly, DeeDee, Connor, Braydon, Nate, Cormac, Nathan, Ray, Mallory, plus others who prefer to not be named.

Many parents, grandparents, aunts, uncles, guardians, and others offered ideas, shared concerns, flagged real-world issues, and graciously shared their families' solutions to digital (and analog) problems. In particular, I'd like to thank Felice Bisby, Joyelle Brandt, Moira Bridgman, Sam Brulotte, Rebecca Coleman, Valerie Crocker, Kimmy Dean, Megan Fox, Angela Hemingway-Adam, Chef Nathan Hyam, Faye Luxemburg-Hyam, Vicki McLeod, Vandhana Misri, Sean Moffitt, Shelley Neill, Kim Plumley, Peggy Richardson, Sean Smith, Janeen Hynd Tronnes, and Eileen Velthuis.

My Master of Education cohort at Simon Fraser University was extraordinary. Together we embraced the issues and opportunities for education technology and learning design (ETLD) with passionate debate and supportive problem solving. I am honored to call Mark Biggar, Trevor Cheng, Todd Goodman, Ryan Hong, Jeff Lynch, Jessica Matthews, Stu Mitchell, Lukas Morel, Trevor Rosencrans, and Kim Sandhu both friends and colleagues. And an extra thank you to the ETLD professors I studied with: Kevin O'Neill, Engida Gebre, John Nesbit, Paula MacDowell, and Allan MacKinnon. Their expertise, research, and encouragement have made me a better teacher.

I also want to express my deep appreciation to the teachers who shared their thoughts, expressed concerns and frustrations, and demonstrated time and again their commitment to supporting the next generation of digital citizens.

Introduction

You live in a digital world. We all do. Every adult has to navigate technology and data daily. Even if you've eschewed technology in favor of an analog life, you'll still use technology to pay for your groceries, call your best friend, buy a transit fare, and fill your prescriptions.

Children and teens growing up today must prepare to function in that digital world. The digital skills they need will partly be day-to-day, practical skills such as shopping online, questioning fake news, and connecting with friends through social media. They will also need digital skills to be part of the future workforce. Increasingly, all jobs require some degree of computer skills and digital communication savvy. Artists sell their creations through online shops. Fishermen (and women) must weigh, inventory, and certify their catch for commercial sale. Myriad jobs in agriculture and manufacturing, service industries, retail sales, and office jobs all require digital skills.

To learn digital skills, children and teens need to see technology in use and have opportunities to try it out firsthand. This happens through observation of modeled behaviors and step-by-step demonstrations of specific skills from both peers and adults. And youth are not afraid to jump in and figure how to use a device through trial and error. Your four year old probably already knows how to navigate apps on your iPad and your teen can communicate through private messaging on Snapchat at lightning speed.

As parents and teachers, it's our responsibility to nurture digital citizens who can, eventually, be fully functioning adults with the problem-solving skills and confidence to tackle any technical situation. Youth learn to research instructions on pretty much anything they need to know "how to." And they learn when to call for help from peers, parents, or teachers if their online search doesn't provide the answer they're looking for. Critical thinking, problem solving, and confidence building are key goals of schools today. Similarly, youth are learning social skills, self-regulation, and responsibility at home. In the best cases, lessons at school echo lessons at home and vice versa. Wherever digital skills are needed, parents and teachers have to take responsibility for raising the next generation of digital citizens.

As a parent or teacher, you may be daunted by this responsibility. Digital information from social media to professional data sets and technology like laptops and mobile phones are constantly changing at a rapid pace. It can be hard to keep up for your own needs, let alone figure out what issues might be impacting youth in your life.

Add to that some terrifying headlines and school presentations that focus on the negative aspects of the internet. Cyberbullying, child pornography, and luring fuel many parents' nightmares. Happily, a longitudinal study conducted at the University of Calgary discovered that these risks seem to be decreasing. CBC News' Ramona Pringle reported, "Having summarized data about over 50,000 youth aged 9 to 17 from existing studies released between 1990 and 2016, the researchers found that, on average, one in five youth have seen unwanted sexual material online and one in nine have received online solicitations.

"But while those numbers are disturbing, the risks have actually decreased. In other words, we're getting better at keeping kids safe online." ("How much online porn do children see unintentionally? Less of it than 5 years ago," *CBC News*, July 4, 2018).

It's important to acknowledge that these are serious issues that must be addressed. But, I argue, an increasing number of families and schools are trying to help kids figure out the basics and best practices in their digital lives. In this book, you'll read lots about the issues and strategies to help you tackle them. You'll also read about the worrying headline topics and find related resources for help, but this book puts emphasis on preventative and practical digital life skills that parents and teachers can help foster in youth today.

Often, parents hear the message that we should keep our kids offline or off screens or off the computer. But this isn't a practical way to protect our children from the perils of technology and the internet. Instead, we've got to teach them how to live with technology. Only with guidance can they develop healthy digital life skills. And they're going to need the freedom to make mistakes and learn from them. Parents can rest easier if they know those mistakes are being made with parental and school supports that reinforce what could have been done differently for a better outcome.

Teachers welcome parents' support in the goal of fostering healthy digital life skills. Lessons at home support lessons at school. Neither parents nor teachers can fully inform and inspire children and teens to be model digital citizens. It's too big a task for any one adult. As Hillary Rodham Clinton said, "It takes a village."

Today's youth have access to more technology and information than any previous generation. And when we talk about youth in this book, we're talking about children and teenagers aged 11 to 18, not their younger siblings who need different supports to navigate technology and the internet. This book focuses on the tween and teenager years. The advice herein is for those guiding that transition from childhood to adulthood; the formative years when boundaries are tested, lessons are learned, new experiences are attempted, and, eventually, adult-level skills are mastered.

Youth need age-appropriate guidance to help them navigate the internet, online communication, digital file management, and more. Ideally, that guidance comes from knowledgeable parents and teachers but not every adult knows what guidance to offer. In some cases, teachers are tech savvy and can teach curriculums filled with digital media, data technology, and online communities. Similarly, some parents are digitally savvy and can offer guidance to help their child live a rich and rewarding digital life. However, there are many parents and teachers who have limited or incomplete knowledge to pass along.

Youth and digital is a big topic, one that both parents and educators want to get right. Yet, we're bombarded by headlines that offer biased or incomplete views of research on the subject. In my view, you're all trying to do the best you can just as I am in my role as Mom. Know that I'm in the trenches with you learning what works for my family on a day-to-day basis. And some days are better than others for all of us.

As an aside, my own experiences with computer technology began when I was about ten years old. My parents, especially my father, were willing and able to provide my brother and me with a home computer starting with the TI-99/4A and later Interact, Commodore 64, and Tandy 1000 TRS-80 home computers. Happily, the laptop I'm using to write this book is faster, lighter, and more portable than any of those predecessors. Growing up, we used the computers to play games (my favorite was *Hunt the Wumpus*) and write school essays while constantly honing our negotiation skills as my brother and I took turns at the keyboard. This early exposure piqued my academic and professional interests in technology and digital communication. As I've lived with technology since the early 1980s, I have a fairly unusual user experience as I reflect on my own years as youth and contrast them to my current years as parent and teacher.

This book is for those parents and teachers seeking help. *Digital Life Skills for Youth* is for anyone who wants to be a positive guiding influence on the next generation of digital citizens. General concepts such as digital citizenship and reputation management are discussed. Also included are core skills areas where youth need to develop competencies in order to function in today's job market. Your child or teen needs age-appropriate core skills, social skills, study skills, and safety skills to thrive in their digital life. This book provides relevant information and resources to help you nurture digitally savvy youth.

My research for this book offers insight into many of the issues and hopes to share welcome, sensible, research-based, real-world guidance that can be put into action for most families and classrooms. It's not a prescriptive, one-size-fits-all solution. Rather, you'll read a range of solutions that can be adapted depending on your youth's unique interests, skills, and maturity, moderated by your family and community values. And I've interspersed information about mental health issues such as anxiety and depression to reinforce the need to pay attention to youth mental wellness.

1. Guidance for Parents

Parents have a lot to teach their kids on the journey from infant to adult. There are the basics of hygiene, eating well, physical activity, and sleep. Add to that more complex lessons in interpersonal relations, politics, personal responsibility, and self-regulation, to name just a few. Being a parent is a huge job and digital life skills are an added layer in many aspects of growing up. How to proceed is a personal decision.

Anecdotally, parents fall in three broad categories when it comes to kids and technology. There are parents who restrict digital completely; parents who allow a digital free for all; and, mostly, parents who know some guidance and modeling are necessary to raise digitally aware children into fully functional digital citizens. An awareness of that need isn't enough. Parents require digital skills themselves to be able to model best behaviors, set limits, and provide an environment where digital curiosity is okay and mistakes are tolerated as teachable moments.

"I'm intent on introducing my kids to experiences that begin to prepare them now and make them capable today. I think it's important that they have to learn by trial and error while we are nearby, so they can learn for themselves what they are made of." wrote Chip Gaines in the Fall 2018 edition of *The Magnolia Journal*. While Mr. Gaines is talking about introducing his five children to tools and tasks on the construction job sites that fill his workdays, I argue his statement is equally valid for digital skills. We've got to introduce, coach, mentor, and monitor youth as they find their way online. Over several years, they gain the skills they need.

Teaching digital life skills is a further extension of parenting overall. It's not a special type of parenting that requires a different approach than all your other efforts to raise your kids. Yes, the technology may be new to you and your kids but you're still raising wonderful human beings along the way. As Robyn Wilder writes in her article about Philippa Perry, a British psychotherapist, author, and journalist, "Perry's book posits gently but firmly that being a parent isn't a chore, duty, or something to be 'hacked' at all, but a relationship to invest in and nurture — and one that will pay dividends in the long term." ("Philippa Perry: 'Listen carefully, parents — and don't despair'," *The Guardian*, March 10, 2019). I argue the digital life skills you develop in yourself and your kids will help nurture your relationship for a lifetime.

In my personal journey as a parent, the parenting expert I turn to more than any other is Ann Douglas. Her latest book, *Happy Parents, Happy Kids*, (HarperCollins, 2019), offers detailed research and leadership when it comes to the positive impacts of a happy family, one that nurtures and supports both parents and kids over a lifetime. She writes, "The future needs your kid: a happy, healthy adult who is capable of navigating life's challenges and seizes upon ... opportunities that we can't even begin to imagine today." Ann's words echo my own reasons for writing this book. We are raising the next generation of digital citizens and they are going to need to know how to navigate the digital life. So, let's show them the way in a safe and nurtured environment, as best we can. And preserve the serenity of family life, as much as we can, along the way.

My practical approach to technology in family life is supported by research. As Anya Kamenetz wrote in the *Columbia Journalism Review* (November 5, 2018), "there's existing research on parental attitudes and successful parenting strategies regarding digital media. You can help your kids learn via digital media, experts say, and use it constructively. You can help manage and moderate their use." Further, Jordan Shapiro wrote, "Your job as a parent is not to stop unfamiliar tools from disrupting your nostalgic image of the ideal childhood … Instead, it's to prepare your kids to live in an ethical, meaningful and fulfilled life in an ever-changing world, " (*The New Childhood: Raising Kids to Thrive in a Connected World*, Little Brown, Spark, 2018).

That said, when I advocate for youth to have access to technology and learn to use it well, I temper that recommendation with a strong caution about the potential impacts on youth's mental health. As Jingjing Jiang wrote for the Pew Research Centre "The ubiquity of social media and cellphones and other devices in teens' lives has fueled heated discussions over the effects of excessive screen time and parents' role in limiting teens' screen exposure. In recent months, many major technology companies, including Google and Apple, have announced new products aimed at helping adults and teens monitor and manage their online usage." (www.pewinternet.org/2018/08/22/how-teens-and-parents-navigate-screen-time-and-device-distractions/, accessed August 22, 2018). Too much screen time is detrimental for users of any age. Part of the lesson parents and teachers must impart is how and when to unplug, and how to recognize and counteract the ill effects of too much technology.

This book is an opportunity to fine tune your parent radar. You'll learn about digital issues and technological considerations and then decide how to apply them in your family. You'll also learn things such as texting abbreviations and the sexual interpretations of emojis (see the back of this book or use the downloadable kit; instructions for access at back of book) to help you decipher and understand youth's online communication. The age of your children, their maturity, your family's financial position, and more will influence how you introduce and moderate technology use. It's a personal decision and this book is designed to present the options based on best practices and research. This book is not a one-size-fits-all prescription for every family.

Instead, you'll discover a range of approaches that can be personalized to suit your situation.

To help you figure out your approach to digital life skills, use the Digital Qualities Worksheet (see Sample 1) to think about what's important to you and the ways that your family operates. By understanding your approach, you'll be able to decide how to approach the digital skills in this book with your kids in a way that suits your family. All of the worksheets used in this book are available on the download kit for you to print off or type in, as you need. Again, see the back of the book for instructions on how to use the download kit.

Parents today are on a pioneer expedition. We're figuring out parenting issues influenced by technology in real time. As a parent, you are the expert on your child. By reading this book, you'll prepare yourself to guide youth in your care wherever their journey takes you. I'm on that journey with you as Mom to my amazing son, a child who has had an internet use contract, updated annually, since he was four years old. This year we'll write the tenth edition of that contract to reflect his age-appropriate use of social media and a mobile phone. I'll tell you more about internet use contracts in a later chapter. It's just one of many tools in this book your family might adopt in your digital journey.

Let's work together to raise a digitally aware next generation of digital citizens.

2. Support for Teachers

I've written this book with both parents and teachers in mind. I have tremendous respect for today's teachers. You may be one of those teachers faced with the daunting task of classroom management with the distractions of personal electronic devices, in addition to playground politics or teen angst. You may also be taking on new curriculums that reflect the broader influence of technology today. After all, school is designed to prepare students for their future careers.

Many teachers are now being asked to teach digital literacy and digital citizenship. Some schools integrate the lessons into familiar subjects like social studies or language arts. Other schools are adding new courses focused on digital life. And a lot of schools are blending these two approaches. Often, technology decisions are made based on budgets, fundraising, donors' directed gifts, or grants. And some schools have while others have not.

Sample 1
Digital Qualities Worksheet

Date: February 21st	
Use this worksheet to explore and record the digital qualities that matter to you and your family. Whether at home or out in the community, think about the values, conventions, and exceptions that are important for youth to master as they learn digital life skills.	
Number of youth: 2	
Age(s) of youth: Laura (15), Eddie (13)	
What, if any, unique conditions apply to your family? (e.g., youth who is hearing impaired; youth who is gifted, etc.)	Laura struggles to self-regulate screen time.
What is your personal comfort level with technology? Do you love it or hate it? Do you find technology intuitive or do you struggle to master it? Are you willing to use it in your family?	Willing to use it. Intuitive to use.
What is your financial situation? What can you afford in terms of technology purchases, internet service, and mobile phone plans?	To save costs, my kids' mobile phone have no data. They can use Wi-Fi.
What technology is currently available in your home? Are these shared devices or does each family member have their own? What, if any, technology would you like to add?	Laura has her own laptop. Eddie uses a shared computer. Both have mobile phones.
In terms of technology use, describe the maturity, ability, interest, and potential for each youth in your household to thrive with technology.	Laura does OK if she focuses on her work. She is easily distracted by social media. Eddie works well with technology in our home.

Sample 1 – Continued

How will you monitor youth for mental wellness? What atypical behaviors must be exhibited for you to intervene? What resources are available in your area if youth need professional support?	I will make one-on-one time with each of my kids a daily priority. If a crisis emerges, I will call 911 or the nurseline or text CONNECT-TO-686868
What is your approach to screen time? Are you setting strict time limits or making screens available based on other criteria (e.g. sleep, chores, fitness, social)? Do you allow more screen time to accommodate a heavy homework load or to support a youth pursuing interactive or creative pursuits online?	I set fairly strict time limits with exceptions for extra schoolwork and to pass the time on travel days.
Do your family rules about technology change in special circumstances? What if an elder is in hospital or your family takes a vacation?	See above.
What are your youth's school requirements for technology? Must they bring a personal laptop to class?	Laura must bring a laptop to class. Sometimes Eddie takes his cell phone to school.
What are school policies about technology? Do they align with your family's approach? If not, note the differences.	School doesn't allow mobile phone use during class time.
Additional notes	

The addition of lessons in digital skills has been a challenge. Teachers are highly trained in numerous subject areas. While they participate in ongoing professional development, they may not have ready access to in-depth training on digital issues and technology. And they may not want to invest time and money to return to university or college for further training.

Remember that, in learning design, technology isn't always something that requires electricity. Paper and pencil are technology. Chairs and tables are technology. A chair and carpet for story circle are technology. And, depending on the lesson, a single computer with projector and screen are all the technology needed. Or, perhaps, your lesson requires each student to have a personal electronic device be that a mobile phone, tablet, or laptop. While this book focuses on things like mobile phone etiquette, computer office skills, and social media savvy, it's important to remember that classrooms don't have to rely on devices all the time.

Yet, reasonably, parents, teachers, and industry want school to prepare students for their future roles in the workforce. Business advisor Chris Brogan expressed this well when he wrote, "With all the shifts in technology, why aren't we prepping people to learn how to interact, how to query, how to do all that will be required to link together and interpret and sift through all this information? " ("It's Time to Rethink What People Need to Learn," ChrisBrogan.com, accessed May, 2019.) Which highlights that learning to use today's technology isn't the full goal. Rather, we want to raise digital citizens who can take what they learn today and expand it to include the things they'll need to know in the future.

Add to that, many teachers have been advised for a decade or more by their employer or union to avoid using social media. As such, they have limited or no experience with these tools. In some cases, long service teachers demonstrate reluctance to take on new approaches and topics. There are further challenges when a school has raised money for a class set of iPads or a computer classroom. These devices need regular updates and inevitably a class set will include a few non-functional units on any given day turning teacher into tech support. In combination, these conditions can make it challenging for the willing teacher to champion digital in their school.

Those teachers that add digital must do so amidst the complex mix of academic, social, and emotional realities of their school communities. In many school districts, digital is considered an add-on subject. Instead, I suggest you frame it as an integrated element in existing lessons. For example, teachers might add heart-rate monitors to physical education class. Similarly, a shop teacher might use a computer-based drafting program. Math classes might use videos to explain concepts. (See Khan Academy for examples.) Language arts classes might use word processing and presentation software. This book presents a variety of the issues and lessons that must be imparted to future digital citizens. Teachers should feel free to adopt or extrapolate the elements that work for their curriculum and school communities.

To help teachers understand and share the approach to digital skills they want to see in their classroom or school community, there is a Digital Teaching Worksheet, seen in Sample 2 and available on the download kit. Use this worksheet to think about how much digital you'll include in your lessons, what your school or school district rules are about students with personal devices, and more. By understanding your desires, you'll be able to decide how to approach the digital skills in this book with your students in the context of your school or district regulations.

And while we're talking about social and emotional realities, let's pause to acknowledge that technology impacts the mental wellness of both teachers and students. Battles over screen time, discipline for unauthorized technology use, negative impacts of unmonitored social media at home, and much more all impact the classroom environment. That collective frustration, anxiety, loneliness, and other negative emotions can be a lot for a teacher to manage both for themselves personally, and for the students they teach.

I'm empathetic to the work that elementary, middle, and high school teachers undertake. While I teach at the postsecondary level, my academic background includes a Master of Education degree from Simon Fraser University, class of 2018. My cohort focused on education technology and learning design (ETLD). Conversations with my classmates, mostly elementary and high school teachers, were an inspiration for this book. And the research and study I participated in have informed my thoughts to support teachers teaching digital life skills to youth. Plus, as an aside, my mum was a teacher for more than three decades, who worked in elementary schools throughout her career. Teacher career politics, school district administration issues, and technology challenges were frequent topics of conversation at our family dinners.

3. Schools and Communities Working Together

Parents, teachers, and others who influence children and teens throughout the growing up years, have to work together to educate and inspire youth emerging as digital citizens. In order to pass on any digital knowledge, you need to understand it yourself. It takes a complex set of skills, social customs, and security considerations. And keeping up to date on the latest options and best practices makes it even more complicated. With this book, you'll expand your knowledge and be better prepared to guide the youth in your home or at your school.

Part of the challenge for teachers and parents is knowing what kids will learn at home and what they will learn at school. There's no obvious divide like there is between toilet training at home and algebra lessons at school. Parents and teachers are regularly on the frontlines with children and teens. Working together as a community, you can establish and normalize social conventions around the use of technology and digital skills by modeling best behavior and setting the tone for what's acceptable.

Community standards can also respect that every family will have its own approach, just as every school will create digital rules that work for the circumstances of each school community. It's essential that we respect differences from the digitally disconnected to the hyperconnected and everything in between. The overarching goal is to help youth gain new digital life skills, at the right pace and with purpose.

Add to this a requirement to find ways for youth with diverse needs to access technology and the internet in ways that support them. This varies based on maturity and experience. Each child, each teen grows and evolves at different pace for different developmental markers; moral reasoning, socialization, impulse control, and more. In addition, designations such as gifted, autistic, learning disabled, dyslexic, or other exceptional labels must be considered to acknowledge and adjust for neurodiversity. This impacts how and when kids are ready for each

Sample 2
Digital Teaching Worksheet

Date: March 22nd	
Use this worksheet to explore and record the digital qualities that matter in your classroom. Use it as a guide to help you design lessons and learning activities that support youth learning to master digital life skills.	
Grade level(s): 8	
Class size: 29 students (6 with IEP)	
What is your personal comfort level with technology? Do you love it or hate it? Do you find technology intuitive or do you struggle to master it? Are you willing to use it in your lessons?	Happy to use it but frustrated when it takes away for lesson time.
What is the school's policy regarding technology in the classroom? Do you have autonomy to make different rules apply to your students while they are in your classroom?	No tech from first bell to last bell unless teacher permits in class use as part of the lesson.
What technology resources are available in your classroom? Do you have a computer, projector, and screen?	Projector, teacher's computer Time weekly in computer lab for class activities.
What technology resources are available in your school? Is there a computer lab or class set of laptops?	Computer lab
What technology resources do your students bring to class? Are they required to have a mobile phone, tablet, or laptop? Do your students have the resources to provide their own technology?	Students bring their mobile phones to class only when instructed to do so for the lesson.

Sample 2 – Continued

Are your students learning in a blended environment? What technology will they use in class and what will they access online?	Not a blended environment.
What accommodations does your class require? What technology considerations appear in their individualized education plans (IEP)? What types of unique abilities must you consider in your lesson planning?	1 student with dyslexia 3 ELL students 2 students with ADHD
Does the prescribed curriculum give you opportunities to incorporate digital skills into the lessons? Do you teach specific digital curriculum? Are you teaching an inquiry model that can incorporate technology?	Yes, I teach digital citizenship classes and include technology in other subjects.
If needed, what disciplinary measures are authorized and appropriate for your students?	Mobile phones impounded for misuse. Escalate to principal, if needed, per school district policy.
Additional notes	

next stage of digital skills. And it's important to note that chronological age does not indicate the same level of readiness. What one 13 year old is able to manage might be more or less than another 13 year old.

The American Academy of Pediatrics guidelines (https://www.aap. org/en-us/Documents/ppe_document108_en.pdf, accessed May, 2019) recommend that youth's screen time be planned in the context of other important activities. Their default recommendation is two hours of screen time per day for those 13 through 18 years old but they acknowledge that some youth will get more time onscreen. They go on to recommend that families focus on the balance of other activities. If the youth gets a full night's sleep, an hour or more of physical activity, meals with family members, and some unplugged time each day, then the amount of screen time can be adjusted. Each family will do this based on the youth's volume of homework, social interactions with friends online, and other screen-time activities in combination with their household's rules and attitudes about screen time. For some families, this means unlimited screen time while others use strict time limits. Most families fall somewhere in between where there are limits but they vary based on the needs, abilities, and maturity of the child in combination with parent's monitoring of healthy lifestyle habits. And for some families the rules change between weekdays and weekends. Vacation also introduces variations with more or less screen time based on the family's wishes and the type of vacation.

As an example, while I write this, it's a rainy Sunday afternoon. I can hear my son talking to his friends on Discord while they cooperatively build a fleet of ocean vessels in *Roblox*. The conversation is lively and filled with social play just as there would be if they were in the same room. But, given the weather and that I'm working on this book, he'll have a long stretch of screen time today. I'm unconcerned because he sleeps well, eats nutritious meals (and he made me breakfast in bed this morning!), and he's physically active for two or more hours most days of the week.

As communities collaborate to support youth emerging as digital citizens, it's important to acknowledge that there are a variety of adults who influence youth and that they are equally influenced by their peers. Youth will see digital behavior modeled by parents, teachers, coaches, spiritual leaders, neighbors, retail clerks, transit workers, and other adults they meet in the community. In turn, as youth move from an attachment to their parents to an attachment to their peers, their friends (and, possibly, enemies) at school will influence their understanding of digital behavior.

Whether parent, guardian, teacher, or other community member in a position to model digital behavior, your goal is to help raise a child who is able to function effectively in a digital world so that they are ready to both join the workforce and take responsibility for all aspects of their lives as adults. In the chapters ahead, you'll find digital skills grouped in four categories core skills, social skills, study skills, and safety skills.

You'll notice safety skills are just one of the categories. Here we'll touch on the risks of being online and using technology. Rather than offer scare tactics (as many social media educators have done in recent years), you'll focus instead on teaching youth the skills to prevent them from getting into trouble. You'll also find resources to help you get help if something awful should happen to a child or teen in your life. While cyberbullying, luring, and pornography make attention grabbing headlines in the news, most families and teachers are struggling with mundane but vital issues like screen time, reputation management, and securing privacy. Adopt a healthy caution around these issues but try not to let your fear prevent you from helping youth learn healthy digital habits.

Digital Citizenship

If we think of the internet as a place, not a thing, we can extend the metaphor and think of the internet as a worldwide community in a virtual place. While that place has no street address, it is a place where people can gather no matter where they are in the world. A friend in Adelaide is just as reachable as a friend in Chicago, keeping in mind the time zones, of course. It's a place where we gather in a technology-rich, digitally driven environment that comes with opportunities and responsibilities.

Anyone who goes online participates in this global community and, by extension, becomes a citizen of the internet. As a digital citizen, you participate online within a set of ground rules or acceptable behaviors. What's OK in one part of the internet will not be OK in another part so it's important to learn how to connect with people and information under different virtual conditions. These customs of digital citizenship evolve over time to reflect people's experiences and the technology's ever-expanding capabilities.

At its simplest, a digital citizen is someone who uses information technology as they go about their daily activities.

Many people write about digital citizenship. In fact, my son's class recently had to write an essay on the topic and dozens of Grade 8 students had to contemplate what this means to them. Sean Crocker, age

12, wrote, "You become a digital citizen by choice, not genetically. Being a good digital citizen means that, among other things, you know responsibilities from irresponsibilities."

The Office of the eSafety Commissioner in Australia promotes a three-pronged definition: engage, know, and choose. Their work contends that anyone who visits the internet is a digital citizen and recommends that digital citizens "Engage positively. Know your online world. Choose consciously."

Mike Ribble, Director of Technology for the Manhattan-Ogden Public Schools in Kansas, offers a parallel view. He defines digital citizenship: "Digital citizenship is the continuously developing norms of appropriate, responsible, and empowered technology use." (www.digitalcitizenship.net, accessed May, 2019). Mr. Ribble's work on digital citizenship provides a detailed framework of nine elements with an overlay of three overriding principles: Be safe. Be savvy. Be social. The nine elements deeply explore the complex array of skills and knowledge needed to function fully as a digital citizen. These include access; commerce; communication and collaboration; rights and responsibilities; health and wellness; fluency; security and privacy; etiquette; and law. These overlapping and intersecting elements collectively provide a rich and complex definition of digital citizenship. You can read more about them at www.digitalcitizenship.net/nine-elements.html.

Teachers, I encourage you to explore the information and resources available from Mike Ribble. His website includes a functional and helpful digital citizenship progression chart that enumerates the nine elements by grouped grade level including notes on the cross-curriculum connections. www.digitalcitizenship.net/dc-progression-chart.html

However you describe digital citizenship, youth need to learn the rules, customs, and responsibilities over time. And, along the way, they're going to make mistakes and learn from those mistakes. And, yes, they may make the same mistake over and over before they learn. That's part of growing up. But, if we provide them with guidance we can help them be safe online while they enjoy their place in the global online community.

This book explores a variety of skills that youth need to learn as they grow into their role as digital citizens. The skills are broadly grouped in four categories — core skills, social skills, study skills, and safety skills. While written in a particular order in the book, parents and teachers should introduce and mentor skills as needed by the youth around them. To help you keep track of your efforts, Sample 3 shows you the Digital Life Skills Master Checklist also available on the download kit. Make a copy of this list to note skills your youth knows and the ones you want to support them in next. You'll revisit this checklist in Chapter 6.

1. Acceptable Behavior

When and where to use technology is a hot topic. Every family and every school have different rules for what works for them. Some feel that anytime is a good time while others feel that it should be heavily regulated with strict time blocks for access to technology and the internet. As youth figure out digital life skills, they learn when and where they are allowed to get connected and they figure out strategies to circumvent the rules they've been asked to follow.

In my opinion, neither the free-for-all nor the heavily restricted models are effective with youth. Given access to technology without restrictions, they have fewer opportunities to learn acceptable behavior. Overly restricted youth suffer the same difficulty. That said, the degree to which youth can self-control their screen time and web surfing varies depending on their age, maturity, and circumstances.

So how do parents and teachers proceed? At home, parents set the rules. At school, teachers are in charge. Youth need some parameters to help them figure what they are allowed to do and when. At the same time, society as a whole needs to acknowledge that all digital actions look much the same; head down, thumbs on mobile phone screen. What's less clear at a distance is what a person is doing when they are taking digital action.

Take for example, Gijsbert van der Wal's viral photograph of students on their mobile phones in front of Rembrandt's *The Night Watch* (www.telegraph.co.uk/news/newstopics/howaboutthat/12103150/Rembrandt-The-Night-Watch-The-real-story-behind-the-kids-on-phones-photo.html, accessed May, 2019). When this photo first circulated, the response was a universal outcry that youth were ignoring the masterpiece next to them. However, that response took the moment out of

Sample 3
Digital Life Skills Master Checklist

Date: January 20th

Name: Ann

Youth will be ready for different digital skills at different times. As their skills grow, use this checklist to track their development through the digital skills described in *Digital Life Skills for Youth*. If you like, you could use two different marks for each checkbox — a simple slash (/) to note the skill has been introduced followed, later, by a second slash (\) to turn it into a X once mastered. If desired, add the date, too, so you can see their progress over time.

As with all things in this book, every family and every classroom will vary their approach to support the unique needs of the youth involved. An editable version of this checklist is available in the download kit. Adapt it to suit your situation.

Core Skills

- ☐ Reputation management
  - ☐ Time management
  - ☒ Privacy
  - ☐ Navigation
  - ◩ Communication
  - ☐ Finances
  - ☐ Streaming
  - ☒ Around the house
  - ☐ Physical fitness

Study Skills

- ◩ Setting up accounts
- ☒ Passwords
- ◩ Family relationships
- ◩ Being a good friend
- ◩ School, parties, and social events
- ☐ Notifications and distraction
- ☐ Gaming
- ☐ Influence and influencers
- ☒ Content creation and curation
- ☐ Social media
  - ☒ Snapchat
  - ☐ Instagram
  - ☐ YouTube
  - ◩ TikTok
  - ☐ Facebook
  - ☐ Twitter
  - ☐ Other:

Sample 3 – Continued

Social Skills

- [/] Reading and writing
  - [/] Analog or digital reading?
  - [/] Analog or digital writing?
  - [/] Spelling, spell check and a dictionary.
  - [/] Grammar & grammar check
  - [/] Style guides
  - [/] Citations
- [ ] School communication
  - [/] Messaging and emails
  - [ ] Managing your inbox
  - [ ] Placing phone calls
  - [x] Phone etiquette
- [ ] Note taking
  - [ ] Analog or digital?
  - [ ] Voice dictation
  - [/] Organizing files
- [x] Web search
  - [x] Tools to refine your search
  - [x] Find organic search results
  - [x] Assess quality of website
- [ ] Identifying fake news and bias
  - [ ] Fact checking
  - [ ] Ambiguous language
  - [ ] Context
  - [ ] Types of bias
  - [ ] Verify a story
- [ ] Productivity and organization
  - [/] Notetaking
  - [x] Calendar
  - [ ] Back ups
  - [/] Synchronization
- [ ] Creativity
  - [ ] Writing
  - [ ] Audio
  - [/] Video
  - [ ] Visual art
  - [ ] Other creative modes
  - [x] Consume creativity

Safety Skills

- [ ] Digital responsibility
- [x] Community alerts
  - [x] Social media notices
  - [x] School apps and websites
  - [x] Emergency alert system
- [/] Identity theft
  - [/] Shred your paper trail
  - [x] Password protect your devices
  - [ ] Two-factor authentication
  - [x] Risks of open Wi-Fi
  - [/] RFID "tap" payment cards
  - [/] Email scams
  - [/] Social media risks
- [ ] Navigating nudity
  - [ ] Sexually explicit content
  - [/] Nude photograph requests
  - [ ] Coercion (threats)
  - [/] Document and report
  - [/] No! graphic
- [ ] Cyberbullying
  - [x] What is cyberbullying?
  - [/] Criminal acts
  - [x] Support available
  - [ ] What to do if you are bullied
- [ ] Legal obligations
  - [ ] Mistakes happen
  - [x] Reporting

context, as the students had been examining the painting and turned to their mobile phones to do a complementary learning activity on the museum's app.

Similarly, people will often decry that people are always on their mobile phones while commuting by train or bus and not talking to one another. However, Gary Vaynerchuk countered that assumption of acceptable behavior, with a 1947 photo of commuters reading their newspapers on a subway car. He noted, "every single person, even though they're in a confined space together, aren't paying any attention to each other because they're reading media on a newspaper. The recent version of this is, of course, cellphones and iPads, yet the same people out there who hate change continue to cry foul." (*Medium*, "Technology Hasn't Changed Us," accessed December 28, 2013.)

Another battleground is the family dinner table. As with all digital behaviors, there are a range of acceptable options. For some, the dinner table is an opportunity to come together and talk about the day. Others, perhaps more introverted, enjoy the companionable silence of eating alone-together without devices. Yet, other families gather to eat and consume media on their phones at the same time. We can't assume that this family doesn't communicate at other times of day; this is simply the behavior they deem acceptable at the dinner table. My family has variable rules. When at home, we don't allow devices at the table and enjoy our chance to talk to one another. In restaurants, devices stay put away until we've ordered our food and then go away again when the food arrives. For us, the noise of a restaurant is an impediment to conversation. And we have a third variation when we travel, especially for road trips, where devices are allowed at meals. This is often our only access to internet and we want to connect with media and people during our travels. And we have lots and lots of time to talk in the car when we're back on the road again. As with all things, acceptable behavior varies for meal times and other times.

The digital life lesson is to help youth understand the variations in the rules and ways to learn what behavior is OK in a given situation. Schools will often post device-use policies that are reinforced by teachers, including authorized exceptions, in class regularly. In social situations, youth learn to take their cue from observing what others are doing. If all the adults have their phones out, then the youth may feel they can do the same. If that's not a clear signal, youth can learn to ask what's permitted. Or, choose to follow their own standards of behavior, as needed.

It's also important to remember that youth don't remember a world without mobile phones and the internet. To them, this is how its always been and they don't have any memories to wax nostalgic about a time when there were only 13 television channels and people couldn't be reached 24/7. Their life experience informs their behavior. Even for adults, our behavior is also shifting as we live increasingly digital lives. Author and artist Douglas Coupland cleverly reminds us that 'I no longer remember my pre-internet brain." ("Douglas Coupland: 'I no longer remember my pre-internet brain'," *CNN Style*, January 19, 2018). If adults are struggling to remember, how can we ask youth to live by standards that they have no memory of?

Of course, the impacts of digital living are an ongoing experiment, just as every type of media — books, radio, television — has been before. "[When] it comes to spending a childhood in front of a screen, this generation are like lab rats. The long-term impact is not known," notes psychologist Sue Palmer. ("Why the iPad is a far bigger threat to our children than anyone realizes: Ten years ago, psychologist Sue Palmer predicted the toxic effects of social media. Now she sees a worrying new danger ... " *Daily Mail*, January 27, 2016). This is, in part, why youth need guidance to understand not only what's acceptable behavior but, also, to learn the positive and negative impacts of digital activities.

To do this, parents and teachers must be present whenever feasible. Some will choose to watchdog every online action while others will not pay any attention at all. As usual, I advocate for a middle ground where youth are getting some opportunities to be online unsupervised and to practice acceptable behaviors with technology while also spending some time in discussion with parents and teachers. The amount of supervision a youth needs varies by age, maturity, and other milestones. Parents will know and advocate for what's best for their children while teachers will enforce a standard that suits each class community as a whole.

As parents and teachers observe youth's behavior online, I encourage them to praise the good behavior and to call out poor behavior. Grade 7 teacher Ryan Hong, an active education technology innovator, kindly but firmly rebukes inappropriate student comments on his classroom Instagram account (@MrHongsClass). In one instance he wrote, "You need to secure your account and adjust your language. Thank you for your cooperation! Digital citizenship is important! This is your digital footprint that will remain with you." Calling out bad behavior and offering specific guidance for how to shift to acceptable behavior is a constructive way to proceed. In brief, be kind but firm.

In addition, I encourage you to be transparent about your own digital behavior. Even parents and teachers make mistakes. The key is you have to acknowledge the error and note the teachable moment. Just as you learn from your mistakes, you share the lesson and model for our kids that they can recover from a mistake. Redacted. Apology. Thank you.

2. Access to Technology

One of the biggest challenges for parents is deciding when (not if just when) a child or teenager will have access to technology such as a laptop, tablet, or mobile phone. And there's no one-size-fits-all answer to this question.

Famously, industry leaders from the computer and technology industry are reported to prevent their kids from having access to computers and mobile phones. Household names like Melinda and Bill Gates, Steve Jobs, Mark Zuckerberg, and others are said to ban or restrict their children's use of technology and internet access. The implication in this oft reported news is that these technology insiders know something that average parents do not. While you may want to follow suit and shelter your kids from technology and the internet, I don't see it as a practical solution. Youth are going to need access to technology to complete school assignments, manage their own banking, communicate with friends, and more. Even if a family decides to limit streaming entertainment, social media, and gaming, youth will still need to access devices to learn on. That said, they don't necessarily need a personal device to use all the time. A family computer or a shared tablet might be sufficient, at least to start.

Economics is a key driving factor when it comes to access to technology. For some families, it's a financial restriction. Technology is expensive and with each device costing $500 to $1,000, or more, the expenses add up quickly. Add to that monthly costs for a mobile phone plan that may also include data charges. And if your household has more than one youth, it's a juggle to figure out who will get a device and when. Of course, youth may earn their own money and buy computers, mobile phones, and accessories.

Schools too struggle with the expenses associated with technology. Classroom sets of iPads, computer labs, and laptop stations are a huge hardware investment. On top of that, enterprise level software licenses are required and there has to be dedicated staff available to update, troubleshoot, and otherwise maintain each device.

As schools struggle with these costs, many districts are now asking that parents start providing each student with a mobile device or a laptop when youth are in elementary or middle school and that request becomes a requirement in most high schools. This creates a new variation of the access to technology problem if family resources can't provide the required technology.

In addition to the financial considerations, some families need their youth to have access to mobile devices for safety and security reasons. Today's latchkey kids often checkin with parents by text message to confirm they've arrived at home or school safely. And some homes outfitted with smart home devices require a mobile phone instead of key to enter the dwelling. Older siblings are looking after younger siblings. Families with joint custody arrangements rely on technology to ensure drop-off and pick-up information is communicated to all parties.

And there can be medical considerations, too. For example, children with diabetes may have an insulin pump that is monitored via their cell phone with software that only works when it's connected to the internet. Other students track their peak-flow performance with an app designed to help children living with asthma. In all cases, the mobile phone becomes a vital part of their physical well-being. In other situations, children on the autism spectrum and those with sensory processing differences may need one or more apps to assist their participation in school and after-school activities. Similarly, children with vision or hearing impairment may need a phone or tablet to fully participate in class. The technology helps them amplify audio and enlarge images and, in some cases, it helps them communicate. Youth living in a new place may also need that device to overcome the language barrier with translation apps to help them understand what's going on and to express themselves.

Add to that the challenges when schools embrace or ban personal technology. In some schools, tech is banned from first bell to last bell with the exception of digital lessons sanctioned by teachers in classrooms. The school-wide ban is a common strategy to mitigate the challenges of disengaged and distracted students. It can also help foster in-person relationships with fellow students. And there's a practical limit to the amount of bandwidth a school's Wi-Fi network can process. By limiting personal use while school is in session, the available bandwidth can be used for administration and lessons.

That said, a total ban doesn't prepare youth for real life. You live in a digital age and you need to guide kids and teens to learn self-regulation, privacy protection, social interaction, and other digital life skills. If they have no exposure to real world conditions in school, how can they be prepared for real-world living?

Both at the family level and at the school level, youth need clearly communicated boundaries that reflect the policies of the school. Ideally, these should be communicated in writing. (Later in this book, we'll talk about digital privilege contracts for families.) Schools need to make their policy clear at the beginning of every school year and have both students and parents acknowledge, in writing, that they've been informed of the policy. The policy should note both permissions and restrictions and clearly outline consequences for violating the policy. This establishes clear expectations for acceptable and unacceptable behavior. In general, youth perform better when they understand the details.

Both at home and at school, consequences (the twenty-first century word for punishment) should be incremental and escalating. Kids and teens are learning how to use text messaging, apps, social media, and more. They are going to make mistakes; even adults make mistakes. We're all human. As we raise digital citizens, we want them to seek adult support and advice when things go wrong. Yes, it's reasonable to have consequences but make sure the punishment suits the mistake and be lenient for first time or minor offenses, as suits each youth's developmental stage and maturity.

3. Tricky Tactics

Having made the decision to give your child or teen access to a computer, tablet, or mobile phone, I recommend that you talk to your kids about something I call "tricky tactics." These are the workarounds youth, especially teens, use to hide their digital activity from parents and teachers.

If your child is using social media or other digital tools, they may set up **multiple accounts** on the same service. For example, it's common for youth to have an Instagram account that their parents and teachers know about and a second (or even third) account where they post all the things they don't want parents and teachers to see. Often, teens get caught in this practice when a trusted adult stumbles across the secret account or a friend screen captures a post and shares it. However, a proactive parent can check for "other accounts" within the Instagram app to see if more than one account is active. This multiple account tactic can be used on many platforms from Twitter to email.

Search history can be a rich source of information to get a sense of what youth have been searching for on the internet. Some parents and teachers will elect to peruse browsing histories to get a sense of what youth have been looking at online. Adults should note that portions of browsing history can be deleted so what you see may not reveal all the searches. Savvy youth will also know that they can turn on private browsing in Safari, Firefox, Chrome, and other browsers. (In Chrome it's referred to as incognito browsing.) This prevents the browser from recording the search history. That said, private browsing sessions are still recorded by the internet service provider so there are records of the session from your home or school's IP address. Private browsing also does not conceal any keylogging records, if such software has been installed on a school computer, for instance.

Keeping track of contacts' names, phone numbers, email addresses, and more is one of the most useful functions in a mobile phone or email program. However, there are lots of ways for youth to hide contacts in plain view. **Hidden contacts** might be recorded under a pseudonym, fake name, nickname, slang term, or some other naming convention. In addition, innocent looking emojis are often used to record details about the contact. For example, an eggplant represents a penis while a bunch of grapes represents testicles, both with a sexual connotation. Similarly, a peach represents either the buttocks or the vagina. Within contacts, these emojis are used to mark up a contact's record in a way that might appear innocent to adults. (We'll talk more about the use of emojis in Chapter 3.)

Apps add seemingly endless functionality to our tablets and mobile phones. Many of those apps provide information, entertainment, and social connections. However, youth may try to conceal what apps they are using. **Concealed apps** may be hidden on secondary screens or within folders filled with multiple apps and thus only visible if you swipe through all the available screens and sub-screens. If a youth knows that their apps will be monitored, they may delete unauthorized apps before their phone is audited and then reinstall them after the parent or teacher audits their phone. If needed, check the App Store (iOs) or Google Play (Android) to see what apps have been downloaded for free or purchased on their account.

In addition, there are **vault apps** that hide unauthorized apps inside seemingly authorized apps. Vault apps will look and function like a camera app or calculator app. The secret content inside these apps is password protected and the secret content is only revealed when the PIN is entered. And, should an adult come within viewing distance, simply closing the app will hide its secret contents and return it to the seemingly innocent camera or calculator app.

Youth may try to hide their correspondence by **deleting texts** (and direct messages and emails). So much peer-to-peer communication happens through text messages, it's youth's preferred mode of connecting with friends. However, some conversations may not be for adult eyes. Some families make agreements that no text will ever be deleted and any problem texts will be brought to a trusted adult's attention as soon as possible. That said, if you feel it's necessary you can sometimes view and/or recover texts. Of course, youth sometimes use Snapchat or other tools that delete messages once read. These are irretrievable adding another layer of difficulty to tricky tactics.

Big brother is watching and more than ever before you can use technology to monitor your child's location. However, **location monitoring** is a family choice. Some choose to use it and check regularly to keep track of where their child is. For example, are they at school during school hours? Other families find comfort in knowing that the child made it safely from school to soccer practice, especially if that child is traveling on their own on public transit. In turn, other families turn off location and choose not to have that data tracking logged by the device their child carries. If your family leaves location turned on, be aware that youth sometimes turn off location for periods of time when they want to conceal where they are or where they've been. And, in truth, location monitoring shows that your child's mobile phone is at school. Remember that they could easily leave the phone in their locker and leave school grounds during the school day.

Youth love to take photos and will likely document their day in many ways from selfies to snaps of homework assignments written on a whiteboard. Unfortunately, it's possible that not all photographs will be acceptable. Youth may know what is an appropriate photo and what is not. It's important for parents and teachers to be clear about the boundaries. Yes, it's okay to take photos of the school's baseball team at a game. No, it's not okay to take photos of people on the toilet in the restroom. Sexual imagery is also a solid no (and we'll talk more about that in a later chapter). Even if you've laid out the **rules for photography**, youth may take unauthorized photos and try to hide them from adults. This might happen by moving photos into a special folder that they hope adults won't look at. Or they might delete the photos that break the rules when their phone is audited and then un-delete them immediately afterwards. Pro tip for parents and teachers: Look for the deleted photos folder. Usually photos in this folder are held for 30 days, just in case.

Mobile phones require either an Apple ID or a Google Account in order to access apps and cloud-based services. When a phone is set up, typically it uses one Apple ID or Google Account depending on the phone model. However, youth may disable the **original account**, the one authorized by a parent or guardian, and set up a new account to use the mobile phone account as they like without parental controls.

Youth are savvy and, as they grow up, they are testing their limits and exploring their identity. Many youth won't attempt any of these tricky tactics but some will. If youth know their adult mentors are aware of tricky tactics, this may act as a deterrent. Of course, new tactics are being invented all the time so parents and teachers will be most effective if they keep an open dialogue with kids and teens about what is acceptable and what is not. Later in this chapter, you'll read about digital privilege contracts that include, among other things, an agreement that tricky tactics are not acceptable.

4. Self-regulation

Digital citizenship requires self-regulation skills. As we live and work online, you've got to be able to regulate actions and emotions. And you've got to monitor your offline needs — social, physical, emotional, spiritual — and step away from screens as needed to live a healthy and productive life. But apps and devices are designed to keep us playing, engaging, and living online so it takes tremendous discipline and lots of practice to self-regulate in this way.

As an example, consider this day in the life of a tech-savvy teen. She wakes to an alarm on her mobile phone and immediately checks all social media feeds responding to messages and liking friends' posts as fast as possible. During breakfast, she watches a music concert on YouTube before taking the concert into the bathroom while she showers and does her makeup. On her commute to school, she continues to chat with friends via text message, updates her Tiktok, and snaps some selfies. Once at school, she greets her friends and consults about which selfies to post right up until first bell. In class, she must put her phone away but she sneaks a peek at the notification screen anytime the teacher isn't looking. Authorized tech use in class includes time to research medieval medicine for a social studies project. After school, she continues nearly constant use of her mobile phone until swim practice and then boots up the family computer to do her homework on a larger screen before dinner. Family meals are screen free so she sets her device aside to eat and chat with her family. Once her after-dinner chores are done, she's back on social media until bedtime and even then she continues to check her phone until her Dad notices the telltale glow at midnight and moves her phone to the charging station in the kitchen.

Meanwhile, an adult's day includes technology in similar but different ways. The master bedroom has an old-school alarm clock but Mom is quick to check her social media notifications first thing. She also checks her personal emails before hitting the shower and getting ready for the day. Over breakfast, she uses an app to order groceries the family needs delivered. Once the kids are off to school, she connects her phone to her car via Bluetooth to listen to her favorite playlist and call her sister while she drives to her teaching job. At the desk in her classroom, she uses a word processor to print out worksheets for today's lessons, consults the attendance spreadsheet, and reviews YouTube videos for future lessons. Throughout her work day she continues to check her mobile phone every time a notification comes through. After work, knowing her spouse will feed the kids, she stops for a spin class, connecting her fitness watch to the machines at the gym to log her workout. Once she's home again, she checks in with her family and streams a familiar movie while she handles assorted evening chores before bed. Once in bed, she plays her turn in *Words with Friends* and completes a pixel art drawing before turning off the light to listen to a podcast as she falls asleep.

Do we struggle to regulate how much time we spend on screens and online because it's more convenient to do things digitally? Or does the novelty of doing things the digital way hold our attention and keep us online? Or is it something else?

For sure, technology has become a boredom buster for users of all ages. And many adults get frustrated with the youth in their lives when the younger generation turns to their phone for entertainment anytime they have to wait or seemingly have nothing to do. Yet, many adults do the same thing every day. Kids learn from what they see trusted adults doing. In a sense, we're showing our kids that technology is a replacement for a pacifier or soother.

Mike Vardy, a parent and Founder of TimeCrafting™, reflected on boredom in a recent Facebook post for Productivityist (www.facebook.com/Productivityist/posts/1567670336698929:0, accessed May, 2019), "I'm trying to teach my son that mobile electronics isn't the only way to pass the time when you're waiting. It's proving to be a tough lesson to teach — and one that I need to be willing to get better at myself as well." I share Mike's challenges on this issue as I work from a home office when I'm not teaching. Much of my work can be done on a mobile phone anywhere with an internet connection. I have to work hard to ensure I put my technology aside and give my son undivided attention after school. It's taken me several years but I finally realized that I need a transition routine between work time and parenting time. But, even knowing that, I still have days when I struggle to release the writing and research filling my mind and put down the technology I'm using. My son's now old enough that I talk to him about my struggle when it happens to model how to respond to the struggle he shares in the transition from gaming time to family time.

5. Screen Time

Perhaps one of the biggest battlegrounds for parents and youth is around screen time. Anya Kamenetz put it well when she wrote, "The digital environment is ubiquitous and only getting more so. If our only intervention as parents is to limit screen time, a growing group of researchers argues, we're not preparing our kids to navigate the world as it is." (*The Art of Screen Time: How Your Family Can Balance Digital Media & Real Life*, PublicAffairs Hachette Book Group, 2018).

What was initially a binary decision — screen or no screen — has now become a nuanced decision. Is the child old enough for screen time? Can screens be truly avoided when they are found everywhere in restaurants, shopping malls, and play spaces? What is the consensus on the quality of the screen time? Are math videos and grammar lessons okay? What about live streams or videos of topics of interest like trains or coding? What about learning sportsmanship, teamwork, and resource management within games? What about social connections through social media and real-time communication with parents and guardians? What about the age of the child or teen? What about the sheer fun of watching TV shows and movies? All those "what about" questions make parents' and teachers' heads spin. Yet, every parent and teacher has to make to decision to suit the youth in their care.

Parents calibrate, considering the age of their child, that child's unique abilities and needs, and the rhythm of family life. And, I should note, to a parent you'll always be a child at any age. (Hi, Dad!) The number of mobile phones, tablets, and computers in the family home also factor into their decisions. Fair and equal access amongst youth in the household has to be calibrated because fair isn't always equal. Older youth will need more time on screens to complete school assignments, for example. Younger youth may resent this as they try to emulate their older peers.

So, parents must consider homework use separate from leisure use to support students' academics. They might also calibrate based on social use to connect with friends in contrast with passive use to watch videos. And what if your youth is passionate about their digital interests in photography, art, trainspotting, TED talks, or other infinite topics? That's another layer of consideration to keep in mind.

Sometimes other things are happening in family life where a digital babysitter is needed to get through the day. I write this without judgment as I've been that parent struggling to deal with the needs of adult family members in hospital and hospice while concurrently caring for my son, then of elementary school age. Sometimes, a video or game on the mobile phone is the only solution at hand.

Candace McGuire, who's currently parenting through the teenage years, notes an additional challenge many parents face, "I've read so much about how extended time on social media is not good for teens. But realistically if one has a teen who uses social media for messaging and staying connected to their social network, how does a parent help them set reasonable limits on time spent online?" Ms. McGuire highlights a societal shift. While peer-reviewed studies are being conducted to assess the impact of screen time, the mainstream media headlines

Sample 4
Screen Time Tracker

Date: _December 19th_

Name: _Patricia_

Youth can use the Screen Time Tracker to keep track of their tasks, appointments, and screen time.

In the tasks column, list all the things that must be done at any time during the day, including healthy living habits. In the appointments column, list all the things that must be done at a specific time. Once all the tasks and appointments have been completed, the time remaining is the maximum available for screen time.

In the screen time column, each box in the grid below represents ten minutes of screen time. Shade the boxes to track how much time is spent on screens. If the entire column is shaded, that represents 3 hours of screen time. If desired, edit the grid to include more or fewer hours of permitted screen time.

	Tasks		Appointments	Screen Time
6am	empty recycling	☒		
7am	put away laundry	☐		
8am	check bike lock	☒	chess club	
9am	call Granny	☒	school	
10am	math worksheet	☐		
11am	socials homework	☐		
12am	read chapter 7	☒		
1pm	shower	☒		
2pm		☐		
3pm		☐		
4pm		☐	↓	
5pm		☐	Taekwondo	
6pm		☐		
7pm		☐	Family dinner	
8pm		☐		
9pm		☐		
10pm		☐		
11pm		☐		
12am		☐		

shared on social media don't always incorporate the nuances of the studies. One report might say two hours per day maximum while another says four hours per day won't have any long-term ill effects. The nuances of the research get lost in the social media sharing of the media reports summarizing academic studies.

In contrast, Jenny Anderson wrote, "I enthusiastically set limits on my kids' tech use. Everything I have learned about parenting suggests that kids thrive with boundaries. We remove these boundaries as they get older because our goal is not to make clones but to let them develop into fully actualized and independent humans." ("A philosophy professor argues kids should use more technology, not less," *Quartz*, January 10, 2019). Author and certified parenting coach Robbin McManne uses a variation on this approach. "My kids always want more electronics time and even though we have limits, there are times where I'll let them go over their limit ... I do this because I know they love it, and I like being able to surprise them with more game time. It's not realistic to say yes all the time, which is why limits and boundaries are in place, but when it's possible, I encourage you to do it and see how it fosters closeness, connection, and cooperation between you and your child." (*The Yelling Cure: How to Feel Less Stressed and Get Your Kids to Cooperate Without Threats or Punishments*, self-published, 2019.) So, maybe the key is deciding at what age your tween or teen is ready to have their boundaries or screen time restrictions lifted. (Incrementally.)

I invited Joyelle Brandt, parent, artist and author of *Parenting with PTSD*, to share her thoughts on digital life skills for kids. When it comes to screen time, she had this to say: "Sometimes good self-care as a parent is letting your child have 'too much' screen time so that you can have enough time to yourself to be a half decent parent. Sometimes good self-care is cutting your own self off screen time because you know it is not doing anything good for your mental health. Only you can know. And in this age where we are being inundated with new standards constantly, I think the most important guidelines for you and your family are the ones you create and recreate on the daily, as you tune in to your own experience. What is right for me in this moment? What is the best for your family right now? How will this make you feel? How will this make my child feel? We can take in the information from outside and balance it against our internal company, and make the decision that feels right in the moment. And when we make a mistake, as we inevitably will, there is always tomorrow to start again."

As Joyelle says, the "right" amount of screen time varies by needs in the moment, age, maturity, activity, and more. Babies, toddlers, pre-schoolers, and elementary-school age children have lower limits, according to research. But it's clear that for the youth you're hoping to help by reading this book will have their screen time limits set based on a complex group of factors. And that the so-called "correct" amount of time isn't tied to age alone.

It's not easy to make decisions about how screen time becomes part of lessons at school and family time at home. Practical, social, developmental, and pedagogical factors are part of the decision. Add to that the research of academics, psychologists, and other experts as they weigh in with more to consider. Let's look at some of that research.

Up until 2015, the American Academy of Pediatrics (AAP) recommended that children under age two have no screen time and that older children have no more than two hours per day. Strictly enforced screen time limits were (and are!) hard to implement in many families and screen time became a battleground where parents needed tools. The AAP responded with a set of guidelines for screen time that take into account numerous factors that influence the quality and effect of a child or youth's screen time experiences. Additionally, in the *Washington Post*, Tanya Slavin questioned, "Is our screen-time anxiety more detrimental than screen time?" (May 30, 2016.) A fair question to which many parents and teachers can relate.

Helpfully, Jordan Shapiro summarized these then new AAP recommendations in an article for Forbes.com (September 30, 2015). To give them context he wrote, "these twelve new guidelines seem far more grounded in the current reality of digital life. But when it comes to innovation, technology, and human progress, even the scientific methods can't provide the objectivity needed to escape the psychological burden of our paranoid default settings." In brief, here's an overview of the AAP guidelines that apply to youth, most of which are echoed throughout the advice in this book:

- **Media online mirrors media offline.** The contents of an ebook, for example, will have similar — potentially good or bad — impact to its print twin.

- **Parents remain parents.** The tasks of parenting remain the same whether a youth uses technology or not. You oversee their well-being, safeguard their safety, set boundaries that will be tested.

Parents teach the essentials of kindness, empathy, responsibility, purpose, and much more.

- **You are a role model.** Youth will observe and mimic the technology use patterns adults around them demonstrate. Similarly, they pay attention to online behavior, as well.

- **Quality content and online activity is vital.** While youth are engaged in real news not fake news, interacting with peers online, and watching accurate, informative (or entertaining) videos, that high quality content has a positive effect.

- **Materials vetted by a trusted source are valuable.** The curation process helps improve the quality of the content youth access. And this saves both parent and teacher time and effort.

- **Family engagement matters.** While your youth may be mortified to discover you're on Instagram with them, that interaction is essential. In parallel, interact in person regularly. Conversations over meals or in the car or other times are vital to keep that connection alive.

- **Unstructured, offline time is part of a healthy life.** Get some exercise. Go outside. Simply play. (I'm convinced this is why I enjoy so much time with art pen and sketch paper!)

- **Limits are necessary.** Communicate them clearly and allow youth to be part of the discussion when limits are set.

- **Teens' interpersonal relationships are vital to their development.** As their primary attachments shift from parents to friends, healthy friendships are built and maintained, at least in part, through frequent online communication. For teens, this is okay. Just help them learn acceptable behaviors and online etiquette, too.

- **While technology is everywhere, having tech-free spaces is healthy.** Decide where technology is not welcome in your home (or school) and make all family members (or classmates) adhere to this rule.

- **Mistakes happen.** And that's how we learn. As I wrote earlier, use your own mistakes as teachable moments. Be alert to high-risk behaviors like sexting or bullying.

Of course, your family may approach screen time from a minimalist point of view. As Lisa Armstrong wrote, "one of the most important ways to help kids have a healthier relationship with stuff is to limit screen time. Limited exposure to media means limited exposure to advertising." ("How to Raise a Minimalist," *Real Simple*, November 2018.)

If you do allow screen time, you may still choose to restrict it. This can be done manually or through parental control and monitoring apps. Tools like Net Nanny (www.netnanny.com, for iOs) and Norton Family Premier (https://family.norton.com/web, for Android) are among the top parental control apps. There are dozens more. Similarly, tech savvy parents may block certain sites at their internet router or use a tool like Circle by Disney (https://meetcircle.com) to restrict youth's devices to operate only during certain preset times each day.

I have chosen not to use these apps and devices in my parenting. But I have only one (awesome!) child to monitor and he is high functioning, mature, and willing to comply (most of the time). In part, I made this decision because I wonder if these tools teach youth about how to live with technology. Also, do they teach youth to accept that big brother is watching? Or do they intensify youth's efforts to hide what they're doing online from parents and teachers? Remember what you read earlier about tricky tactics. Even so, I respect other parents' decisions to use these tools because every family's different.

No matter your family (or classroom) approach, it's helpful to know the negative impacts of screen time. While not an exhaustive list, these include:

- Consuming excessive information daily.

- Finding it hard to ignore your devices, if they are nearby.

- Obsessively, checking emails all day and on evenings/weekends and during vacations or unplugged times.

- Feeling unreasonably sad, jealous, annoyed, angry, or depressed after reading social media updates.

- Notifications are increasingly interrupting conversations, meals, and play activities.

- The amount of time you spend looking at a screen often exceeds the amount of time you spend on healthy lifestyle activities such as personal relationships, nutrition, or sleep.

- Negative impact on sleep experienced due to blue light exposure, notifications, and phantom vibrations from devices.

Bottom line: Different youth can cope with different amounts of screen time. Their maturity, communication skills, social connections, and academic needs are all factors as to how much they can handle. Family lifestyle choices and the needs of siblings will also influence what's appropriate. To help parents figure out a healthy amount of screen time, I recommend looking at each youth's life overall. Think about one specific youth and consider these questions:

- Is the youth getting an adequate amount (approximately nine hours) of uninterrupted sleep most nights?

- Does the youth have social connections to peers including some close relationships (best friends)?

- Does the youth get an hour or more of exercise each day?

- Is the youth meeting their responsibilities around the home and at school? Are chores done and homework completed?

- Is the youth attending school on time and prepared for class regularly?

- Is the youth participating in family meals and social occasions?

- Is the youth completing daily hygiene routines? Showers? Flossing?

If the answer is yes to most of these questions, then whatever time the youth has time left over could, in my opinion, be spent on activities they choose whether online or offline. Other parents will disagree and set stricter limits. That's OK. Every family is different.

At the same time, teachers calibrate screen time based on the needs of the class group. A shared experience watching a documentary can provide variety in a lesson. Just as a flipped classroom learning design can allow students to watch explanatory videos as many times as needed to grasp the math or grammar concept being taught. And teachers have to make their screen time decisions based on the overall needs of a large group of children or teens — each of whom has individual experience with digital information.

Overall, know that digital citizens have to learn how to manage screen time, even if they manage it poorly at times.

6. Digital Privilege Contracts

Not every youth is ready to have a mobile phone or play online games. And as kids grow up, they have to learn how to use digital tools and they must develop respect for the privilege that comes with them. Youth should understand that parents provide the trifecta: the device, the access, and the permission. And just because permission has been granted today doesn't mean it's a permanent privilege. Youth have to want it, respect it, and demonstrate their understanding of the privilege in all their actions.

Access to technology and the internet is a privilege. When parents and teachers grant youth access to devices and Wi-Fi, it comes with an implied digital privilege contact. In other words, getting a mobile phone, for example, doesn't come with carte blanche permission for youth to do anything they want with it. I encourage parents and teachers to formalize the terms of use in a digital privilege contract. However, assuming the details of the contract are understood is a recipe for a big mess later on. As Marisa Cohen wrote, "Set the rules the moment you hand over a phone." ("How Much Privacy Should You Give Your Kids?" *Real Simple*, August 2018).

Every family, every classroom, will have a different digital privilege contract. While I can't sit at your kitchen table (or in your staff room) to help you draft yours, I can offer some example contracts to get you started.

To start, decide on the format you want to use. Is a conversation enough or do you need to write some notes? Or do you want to write up something more official and have both youth and parents sign it to affirm that they have read and understand school rules? At home, will every youth in your household have the same contract or will each be customized to their unique needs and abilities?

Many families hold a family meeting when a youth gets access to a new device or matures to a new level of internet freedom. Some parents simply have a conversation while others will prepare a written contract in advance and present it with the mobile phone, for example, on the condition that the youth must agree to the terms of the contract if they accept the phone.

While I encourage you to have a written contract, many families choose not to do so. You have to decide what works for your family and, if you're not sure, then try something and see how it works. If your first (or second or third) attempt is unsuccessful, you can always try another approach later.

Next, decide on the scope of the contract. Does it cover everything from computer access to internet use to mobile phone responsibilities? Or do you have separate contracts for different elements of your digital lives? For example, my son has two contracts. The first is an internet use contract. This has been updated annually since he was four years old. The second is his mobile phone contract which all three members of our nuclear family signed when he got his first (and so far only) mobile phone.

Here's a recent version of Sean's internet use contract in Sample 5; this one was implemented when he was 11 years old. The language is adapted from earlier versions of the same agreement and the agreement has evolved to reflect his increased maturity and digital skill. Each year's revision, comes from a family conversation to update the agreement. I'm sure you'll understand I've changed a few personal details. Also, I share these with his consent and he acknowledges that he might be embarrassed that I've published these for all the world to see! Yet, he's happy to share if it will help other families. The contracts are also included on the downloadable forms kit that comes with this book for you to alter for your purposes.

As Sean has grown up, his internet savvy and digital skills have expanded. At age 13, his father and I agreed he was ready for his own mobile phone. When we presented the phone, he had to sign this contract before he accepted. Unlike the internet use contract, as parents, we drafted the contract in advance. And Sean negotiated revisions we had to initial before he signed at the bottom.

Even if youth buy their own mobile phone or laptop, I recommend that these devices should always be governed by your family's digital privilege contract.

No matter the format or the terms, mutual understanding is key. Make sure to use language that both youth and parents will understand. As you build your contract, include clauses that reflect the digital life issues that are priorities for you as parent (or teacher) and those that are priorities for youth. This ensures both parties have input into the contract.

Social media is filled with memes that highlight potential punishments or consequences. If this approach works for your family, then include the consequences in the contract. Examples include:

Sample 5
Digital Privilege Contract: Internet Use

Internet use contract for an 11 year old

1. Never share your last name.
2. Never share where you live.
3. Never tell if you're going on vacation.
4. Never tell how old you are.
5. Never use curse words or bad words.
6. Never talk about private parts.
7. It's OK to share photos but never send photos of where we are. Also, no photos of private parts.
8. Always tell Mom or Dad if someone asks where you live.
9. Always tell Mom or Dad if someone asks about your private parts.
10. Always tell Mom or Dad if someone asks if you are going on vacation.
11. Ask Mom or Dad before joining the conversation in new, yet-to-be-approved apps.
12. To date, _____ Sean _____ has permission to have chat in the following apps:
    a. iMessage chat with Mom, Aunts, cousins, etc.
    b. WhatsApp with Grandpa
    c. Skype chat with Mom, Dad, or Grandad
    d. Facetime with Mom
    e. *Minecraft* — friends on our *Minecraft* server and those on approved shared servers.
    f. *Roblox*: those on shared servers.
    g. Twitter: private account — can tweet and @reply to both followers and following.
    h. Instagram: private account — can post and @reply to both followers and following.
    i. YouTube: can upload private videos, comment, and reply to comments.
13. Mom or Dad may review chat history at any time to make sure it's kid appropriate.
14. Always use good manners. Be kind. Treat people with respect. Remember you are speaking to a person, not a machine.
15. Turn off geotagging. Don't reveal our location in your data.
16. Headphone volume must be low. Usually four bars. If Mom or Dad can hear your sound, it's too loud. When possible use the decibel limiting headphones or the volume limiter on the iPad settings.
17. "No technology at the table." Must be said in a Scottish accent like Merida's Mom in *Brave*. This rule applies to _____ Sean _____, Mom, Dad, and guests. Only exceptions are doctors on call and Dads who might get a call from their pregnant wives.
18. We agree that ending tech time requires a heads up including a time-specific countdown.

19. On school days, technology is turned off at 8:18 a.m. unless all "getting ready for school jobs" are done.

20. Treat technology gently. Use Otterbox cover on the iPad mini. Don't throw your wireless keyboard on the floor. Headphones are fragile.

21. Clean your screens regularly. Use the "technology wipes" in the bathroom drawer, as needed.

22. Consequences may be enforced if any of the rules are broken. This includes losing technology privileges for an hour, a day, or a week depending on the problem. Per _____Sean's_____ request, the consequences will start small and grow with repeated offenses for the same problem.

Signed _____ (Youth)

Signed _____ (Mom)

Signed _____ (Dad)

Date _____

Sample 6
Digital Privilege Contract: Mobile Phone

Mobile Phone Rules for _____

Dear _____,

Now that you are 13, we think you're old enough and responsible enough to have your own mobile phone. As your world gets bigger, we want you to be able to communicate with us, with other family members, and your friends, too. We've made this contract so that we all understand how you'll use your phone.

And, by the way, your phone number is _____.

Love,
Mom and Dad

I understand:

- [ ] that having a mobile phone is a privilege.
- [ ] failure to adhere to this contract may result in loss of mobile phone privileges.
- [ ] that I am responsible to know where my phone is located at all times.
- [ ] that I am responsible for charging my phone.
- [ ] if I damage my phone – whether intentionally, by accident, or by my neglect – I am responsible for fixing it.
- [ ] that I must clean my screen and headphones regularly.

Texting rules:

- [ ] I will not send rude, mean, or threatening texts to others.
- [ ] I will not use curse words or other bad language in my texts.
- [ ] I will report to Mom or Dad anyone who sends me rude, mean, or threatening texts.
- [ ] I will not text or place phone calls between 9:00 p.m. and 8:00 a.m.
- [ ] I will not delete any messages or photos without permission from Mom or Dad.

Location rules:

- [ ] I will turn off geotagging on my phone, especially for photos.
- [ ] I will leave geotagging on for approved apps including Find My Phone and Google Maps.
- [ ] I will ask Mom or Dad to approve other location apps on a case-by-case basis.
- [ ] I will never share my location, announce where I'm going, or publish vacation plans.

App rules:

- [ ] I will ask permission before downloading any new apps.
- [ ] I will pay for my own apps and in-app purchases.
- [ ] I will never use any "vault" apps to hide my phone activities.

Sample 6 – Continued

Photo rules:

- ☐ I will embrace #postedwithpermission.
- ☐ I will not use my phone's camera to take embarrassing photos of others.
- ☐ I will not send embarrassing photos of my family or friends to others.
- ☐ I will keep my private parts private. I will not take photos of any body part that is normally covered by clothing.
- ☐ I will not ask another person to take photos of their body for me to see.
- ☐ If I receive any photos of private parts, I will report this to Mom and Dad on the same day so that we can file a report with the police. This is important so that we are not charged with crimes.

Mobile phone plan details:

- ☐ Mom and Dad own the phone and are lending it to _____ for ongoing use.
- ☐ Mom and Dad will pay for the first 12 months of mobile phone service. The contract is $20/month plus taxes. After the first 12 months, we'll decide as a family how to pay for the service going forward.
- ☐ I will not go over my plan's monthly limit of minutes or text messages. If this rule is broken, I agree to pay any and all additional charges and understand that I may lose cell phone privileges.

  The plan includes:
  - ☐ Caller ID, Call Forwarding, Call Waiting, Conference Calling, Voicemail 10
  - ☐ 350 local outgoing minutes
  - ☐ 1000 local incoming minutes
  - ☐ 250 in-country long distance minutes
  - ☐ Unlimited Incoming and Outgoing in-country Text and MMS
  - ☐ There is no data on this plan. I must use Wi-Fi or a hotspot for any data needs.

General Rules

- ☐ I will share all passwords and login information with Mom or Dad, and will notify of any changes. These will be stored in a password spreadsheet.
- ☐ Upon request, and without delay, I will sit with Mom or Dad to review my mobile phone activity.
- ☐ I will not bring my cell phone to the family dinner table.
- ☐ I will make sure my phone is turned off when at the movies, in restaurants, care homes, or other quiet settings.
- ☐ I will obey all cell phone rules imposed by my school.
- ☐ I will treat people with respect and remember I am speaking to a person not a machine (except for Siri).
- ☐ Headphone volume must be low. If Mom or Dad can hear your sound, it's too loud.
- ☐ Mom and Dad agree that ending tech time requires a heads up including a time specific countdown.

Sample 6 – Continued

I understand that consequences may be enforced if any of the rules are broken. This includes losing technology privileges for an hour, a day, or a week depending on the problem. Per _____ request, the consequences will start small and grow with repeated offences for the same problem.

Signed _____ (Youth)

Signed _____ (Mom)

Signed _____ (Dad)

Date _____

- Loss of mobile phone privileges for a day/week/month.

- Loss of internet privileges for a day/week/month.

- Chores to earn the Wi-Fi password.

- Take away chargers and only remaining battery life may be used.

- Stricter time limits.

- Shut off Wi-Fi access at the router.

Teachers take a different approach creating a set of rules that will be applied to all students. Often, the school or school district will have permission forms that parents must sign to allow students to access the internet for educational purposes, affirm understanding of social media rules, and so on. See Sample 7.

Beyond family based digital privilege contracts and school agreements, youth have to learn and understand the rules of engagement across the internet. Many online communities have standards of behavior and actions that are unacceptable. The Terms of Service for Facebook, for example, state in clear language that "People will only build community on Facebook if they feel safe. We employ dedicated teams around the world and develop advanced technical systems to detect misuse of our Products, harmful conduct towards others, and situations where we may be able to help support or protect our community. If we learn of content or conduct like this, we will take appropriate action — for example, offering help, removing content, blocking access to certain features, disabling an account, or contacting law enforcement." (See www.facebook.com/terms.) Stimulate conversation with kids and teens about their digital lives by ensuring their understanding of the Terms of Service for any service they use. Here's a list with links to the most commonly used social media accounts today:

Instagram	help.instagram.com/478745558852511
SnapChat	www.snap.com/en-US/terms
YouTube	www.youtube.com/t/terms
Tiktok	www.tiktok.com/en/terms-of-use
Twitter	twitter.com/en/tos
Facebook	www.facebook.com/terms.php

Sample 7
Digital Privilege Contract: Classroom

As part of our learning activities, our class will use technology including mobile phones, tablets, and/or computers. Everyone in our learning community – students, teachers, visitors – is expected to follow our digital rules and conduct themselves as responsible digital citizens. This means you understand:

- [ ] The school code of conduct applies both online and offline.
- [ ] The opportunity to use technology is a privilege.
- [ ] Technology that belongs to the school must be treated with respect.
- [ ] No unauthorized changes to school hardware or software are permitted.
- [ ] That you are responsible for your personal device(s).
- [ ] You will make sure your phone is in "do not disturb" mode in class.
- [ ] Headphone volume must be low. If someone next to you can hear your sound, it's too loud.
- [ ] You will treat people with respect both online and offline.
- [ ] You will not send rude, mean, or threatening messages to others.
- [ ] You will report anyone who sends rude, mean, or threatening messages.
- [ ] Poor digital behavior will result in loss of privileges and repeat offenses will have escalating consequences.
- [ ] Use of the internet at school is for educational purposes only, not entertainment unless explicit permission is given.

By signing below, you indicate that you have read and understood these rules. Please share this document with your parent/guardian and have them sign it, too.

Signed _____ (Student)

Signed _____ (Parent/Guardian)

Signed _____ (Teacher)

Date _____

In addition, hosts of specific communities online will publish terms of service. This might happen within a Facebook group or across numerous social media platforms. In the year when I was writing this book, Meghan Markle married Prince Harry and together they welcomed their first child, Archie Harrison Mountbatten-Windsor. Unusually, the British royal family published Social Media Community Guidelines to try to address the sexual, racist, and discriminatory content directed at the Duchess of Sussex and other members of the royal family. They read, in part, "We ask that anyone engaging with our social media channels shows courtesy, kindness and respect for all other members of our social media communities." You can read the full text here: www.royal.uk/social-media-community-guidelines.

I feel strongly that parents need to feel empowered to parent. In some families, I've observed situations where parents seem unable or unwilling to wield that power that comes with the title Mom or Dad. I'm not suggesting we need a dictatorial parenting approach; rather I hope families will find a balance of power where parents nurture and guide their children online, this vast digital place waiting to be explored.

Mental Wellness

As youth spend more time on screens, there is alarming research that correlates time online with youth depression and suicide. A CTV news report by Ryan Flanagan notes the rise of mental-health related hospital visits. According to data from the Canadian Institute for Health Information (CIHI), there was a 65 percent increase in mental health-related hospitalizations of Canadians between the ages of 5 and 24 from 2006–07 to 2017–18, as well as a 75 percent increase in mental health-related emergency room visits. During that decade, we also saw the widespread adoption of the smartphone (the iPhone was introduced in 2007) and the rise of social media including Facebook, Twitter, Instagram, Snapchat, and other channels. The research shows a correlation rather than causation. In other words, the increase in mental illness happened in the same time period as the increase in smartphone and social media use but we can't say definitively that one made the other happen. Jean M. Twenge, PhD, explored the available research thoroughly in her book *iGen: Why Today's Super-Connected Kids Are Growing Up Less Rebellious, More Tolerant, Less Happy — and Completely Unprepared for Adulthood* (Atria Books, 2018). She, too notes, "Although the rise in anxiety, depression, and suicide occurred at the same time as the rise of smartphones, it makes sense to consider other causes as well." While research continues to investigate the links, Dr. Twenge and I concur that the correlation alone is enough to encourage us all to proceed with alert to the mental health risks of digital life.

Talking about mental health in the context of social media is a good first (and ongoing) step. Sam Fiorella's talk "Social media, Tribalism, and Society's Breaking-Point" at Social Media Camp 2019 was thought provoking for many of us as Mr. Fiorella shared his personal story and related research. The poignancy of his son's suicide is a catalyst to action. By reading this book, you are taking a proactive approach to support the youth in your life.

Social media isn't going away. Technology is here to stay. As parents and teachers, you must help youth in your life learn how to live with it in a healthy, meaningful way. You can't be simply sad or mad about the state of affairs, you must do something. As parent and digital publicist Kim Plumley told me, "We've let the genie out of the bottle and we can't put it back in." So, given this reality, what are we going to do to help kids and teens?

In this chapter, and throughout this book, you'll find every topic represents a range of options that you can consider to support and nurture the youth in your life. Whatever your approach to mental wellness, I hope you adopt one that suits your youth (and yourself!). Not all youth need the same solutions. No matter, children and teens need to know how to integrate the attraction of screens within a healthy life, both physical and mental.

1. Understand the Source

We have to teach youth about the mental health impacts of technology use. Before there is a crisis, parents and teachers need to talk to youth about these risks. And you have to do this knowing that you'll talk about these issues and related strategies over and over never quite knowing if the youth around you are listening. Some will. Some won't.

You'll have to decide whether or not to say "I told you so," or take comfort in the knowledge that you tried to prepare them. The goal is to equip them with tools and techniques that maintain mental wellness and prevent crisis.

Beyond the impact of screen time and its impacts on mental health, tech stress is also a core issue. If a mobile phone or computer doesn't work as expected, the failure creates stress. "[The] causes of tech stress are varied and widespread: slow devices and downloads, crashing computers, missing files, annoying popup ads and forgotten passwords are all contributing factors. "(advertorial, *Ottawa Citizen*, 20 December 20, 2016).

Sleep disruption can negatively impact mental health. The blue light of laptop, tablet, and mobile phone screens disrupts the brain's ability to achieve rest. In addition, social media use patterns can be disruptive. Older generations who read under the covers with a flashlight can relate. Anxiety and other causes also contribute to loss of sleep.

Social conflict and strong emotions can also trigger mental illness. From jealousy to anger to happiness, social media feeds run us through a treadmill of conflicting emotions without any real time to process them. In 2017, my friend Vicki McLeod wrote an article about the impacts of the disorganized and chaotic way information flows into our newsfeeds from our ever-expanding online networks. She noted, "Scrolling through the Facebook newsfeed can be an emotional roller coaster ride. Life and death, tragedy and comedy all flow across our screens at a scale and scope that isn't really possible to consciously absorb, let alone respond to adequately." ("Will Simple Emoji Reactions Reduce Our True Expressions," *Maple Ridge-Pitt Meadows News*, 2017.) Overall, we've got to foster the human, not digital, skills of empathy and understanding.

While death and dying might be heavy themes for youth, loss of life can touch their world when a grandparent passes away or a classmate commits suicide. If youth in your life need digital guidance when someone close to them dies, one of my earlier books, co-written with Vicki McLeod, will be a useful resource. Look for *Digital Legacy Plan: A Guide to the Personal and Practical Elements of Your Digital Life Before You Die* (Self-Counsel Press, 2019).

2. Recognize the (Hidden) Signs

Mental illness sometimes triggers behaviors that signal the struggles a person is facing. Simply put, behavior is communication.

However, not every youth exhibits behaviors that are observable. If they are in crisis, youth may show no outward signs of distress. Or the signs may be so subtle that even those closest to them don't notice shifts in personal hygiene, sleep patterns, socialization, and other indicators. In isolation, an indicator will not confirm mental illness (nor can a layperson make a formal diagnosis). However, in combination two or more indicators might suggest there is a problem that requires action. Here are some common indicators to keep in mind:

- If youth stop paying attention to their **personal hygiene**, they may stop bathing, getting haircuts, shaving, or brushing their teeth. As a result, they may present with significant body odor or an unkempt appearance, more so than would be considered normal for the teen years.

- If youth abandon their **self-care practices**, they might give up journaling, team sports, or forego other relaxing/recharging activities. In a digital life, do they stop tracking their 10,000 steps a day on their Fitbit?

- If youth change their **sleep** patterns, they might be having trouble falling asleep or staying asleep. This lack of sleep results in fatigue and irritability.

- If youth **withdraw** from their social circle, they might be questioning the value of their friendships or their own worthiness to have friends. They might stop updating their social media profiles and engaging with their friends online.

- If youth exhibit a **change in personality**, a normally cheerful and positive teen might become moody and aggressive. But the changes can be subtle. Of course, parents and teachers also have to calibrate base on their youth's hormone-driven fluctuations.

- If youth adopt more **high-risk behaviors**, they might take up vaping or smoking, try illicit drugs, or explore new sexual activities.

- If youth are angry, they may be under so much stress that their fight or flight response is triggered. Their **anger** may explode to the point that they cannot communicate what has made them angry.

- If youth are calm and then abruptly fly off the handle, they may be experiencing what Brene Brown calls **chandeliering** when long-suppressed hurt and anxiety suddenly comes tumbling out. An unrelated and benign social media post or online video can be the trigger.

- If youth are **overplanning**, they may be trying to regain control by scheduling details for events that need minimal, if any planning.

- If youth are **avoiding** certain tasks, people, or locations, they may be using avoidance to prevent experiencing the person, place, or thing that's upsetting them. For example, a social media argument may have youth skipping school the next day.

While not an exhaustive list, the notes above empower parents, guardians, and teachers to have some ideas of what to look for. It's most important to note that the behavior that's visible may be a mask for some other unfilled need. A teen who yells at a parent might be struggling to overcome their frustration that a SnapChat streak was broken or a misplaced Instagram tag harmed a friendship. Visualize an iceberg with the behavior represented by the ice above the water and the causes hidden in the ice deep below the water's surface.

Use this Recognizing Mental Health Stress Worksheet (see Sample 8). It includes a quick list to assess a situation from a mental health perspective. And there's space on that checklist to add indicators that you see; parents and teachers are experts in nuances of the youth around them.

Also, know that some stress is healthy! Excessive stress that causes changed behaviors, physical discomforts, and/or emotional pain is the problem.

3. Know Where to Find Help

When youth are struggling, they may seek help or adults around them may realize they need support. Knowing where to find that help is vital. And it's important that adults inform youth of the options available as they may not reach out to trusted adults in a crisis. For urgent assistance, go to the emergency room at your local hospital or dial 911 in the US and Canada, or 999 in the UK.

That said, it is not always easy to access formal mental health resources. Often, emergency rooms have no capacity to support mentally ill patients and, once referred, the waitlist to see a clinical counselor, psychologist, or psychiatrist can be a year or more, depending on your community's medical resources. Add to that medical insurance issues and expensive out-of-pocket costs and it gets even harder to get help. These difficulties accessing formal care can exacerbate a mental health condition by delaying both diagnosis and treatment. As a result, families and schools need tools that can be used as first aid, of a sort. You can learn concrete action steps to address smaller issues that can act as first steps to deal with larger issues.

Sample 8
Recognizing Mental Health Stress

Date: _October 17th_

Use this worksheet to assess any technology user. Changes in behavior or habits may indicate a technology user is struggling with anxiety, depression, or other issues. If observed behavior causes concern, seek support and, possibly, medical intervention, as soon as possible. Remember the crisis text line, nursing line, medical clinic, and emergency room are available to you. In a crisis, in North America, call 911; in the UK, 999. This form includes the nine things to watch discussed in the book and three "other" spaces for you to personalize your observations.

Personal hygiene	Self-care	Withdrawal from social circles
Showers regularly Keeping up flossing	Family walks on weekends Journaling nightly	Friendships seem strong
Change in personality	High-risk behaviors	Anger
None observed	Tried vaping and promised never again. Watch this.	Shouting at sister more than usual
Chandeliering	Overplanning	Avoidance
None	None	Tends to do easy chores first.
Other:	Other:	Other:
Overall, no concerns at this time.		

If you can't get to the hospital, or don't feel the situation warrants emergency care, professional assistance is still available. Many states and provinces offer nurse lines for all types of medical inquiries, including mental health. A toll-free phone number will connect the caller with a registered nurse who can triage the caller's question and escalate it to the right resource, including counselors and other mental health workers. Similarly, schools, community centers, youth groups, and more have support available as do religious and spiritual groups.

In the past, it was taboo to talk about mental health. Today, thankfully, conversations around mental health are more common. As the prevalence of mental health issues becomes more commonplace online and offline, some people are seeking special training to help those in their community. Just as many people have a first aid certificate for cuts and broken bones, you can now earn a mental health first aid certificate. The Mental Health Commission of Canada has a Mental Health First Aid program (www.mhfa.ca/) and the Red Cross offers courses in psychological first aid (www.redcross.ca/training-and-certification/course-descriptions/psychological-first-aid/psychological-first-aid). This sort of certification can help you support youth as they learn digital life skills, as well as support other people in your life.

Now, you may not be present when youth are struggling with mental health issues triggered by digital experiences or offline activities; it's good to make sure they are aware that they can seek help on their own. This is especially important as they may be hiding their symptoms from you or simply not present with any of the typical stress indicators. In a time when youth are most likely to communicate through text, rather than phone calls, a text-based support system for mental wellness is a logical and practical support. Crisis Text Line in the United States, Shout's text-based services in the United Kingdom, and the Kids' Help Phone's Crisis Text Line in Canada (and its French language parallel Jeunesse J'écoute) all provide support through text messaging. Early in 2019, the Duke and Duchess of Cambridge and the Duke and Duchess of Sussex announced their financial and public relations support for Shout, "the UK's first free 24/7 text service for anyone in crisis anytime, anywhere. It's a place to go if you're struggling to cope and you need immediate help." Their Royal Highnesses' global fame brought much needed attention to the need for mental health resources for people of all ages and gave visibility to this text-based solution.

Help via text message is available 24/7 through each of these services with trained crisis counselors (usually volunteers) at the ready to provide support and resources. Always, the goal is to defuse a crisis situation and help the youth regain enough equilibrium to overcome the immediate crisis and seek additional support, if needed. I encourage adults and youth to create a contact in their mobile phone for the relevant crisis line number in your country.

United States text Home to 741741	www.crisistextline.org
United Kingdom text Shout to 85258	www.giveusashout.org
Canada (English) text Connect to 686868	kidshelpphone.ca/text
Canada (French) texter Párlez a 686868	jeunessejecoute.ca/texto

While digital life can cause mental distress, technology can also help create an opportunity to reduce the stress of social isolation, another common indicator of mental illness. Natalie Hampton, Founder/CEO of Sit With Us Inc., invented the Sit With Us app (https://sitwithus.io/) as a response to her own social isolation. Through the app, students can find a welcoming table in the cafeteria at participating schools so that no one has to eat alone. Similarly, Danny Brown, Rob Clarke, and Sam Fiorella co-founded The Friendship Bench https://thefriendshipbench.org, a Canadian nonprofit dedicated to mental wellness. Their work includes bright yellow benches placed on campuses across Canada and funding for coordinating assistance on campus. In addition, there is a supporting social media campaign, #YellowisforHello. Simply by sitting on the yellow bench, students indicate that they want to talk.

These are just examples of the many supports available. Contact your local school or public health clinic to get details on supports available in your area. Forearmed with this knowledge, parents and teachers can be prepared if youth learning digital life skills need additional ongoing support or help in a crisis situation.

4. What Else Can Be Done?

Beyond the formal, professional help that's available, parents, guardians, and teachers can take note of the following techniques to help foster healthy digital life skills in youth. Many of these techniques will also help if youth are teetering toward mental illness. Over a lifetime, different circumstances and different stresses will impact our mental wellness. As youth learn to live with technology, online communication, and social media, they must also learn how to cope day-to-day and how to recognize when they need to step away from their screens. In this section, you'll find some methods to help them in their distress at this age and model things they can master for a healthy future, as well.

To start, simply be there for any youth in distress. Sit with them or be available by phone to help them feel safe. A glass of water, a hand to hold, or some other comfort may be helpful. Once they've calmed down, let them know you're available for them. Express your willingness to listen without judgment and a promise to help them. Later, when the youth feels safe, talk to them about their fear, sadness, or other emotion. What happened online that triggered the emotion? What could have been done differently? These questions and more will help them understand what happened and gain confidence to cope with similar circumstances in future. Here are some phrases and questions you might use within this technique:

- I'm here for you.

- Just breathe.

- I see this is hard for you.

- Please be gentle with yourself.

- How are you feeling?

- How can I help you organize a digital break?

- Do you see the consequences of your actions?

- How can I help you?

- Do you need a hug?

Another tactic, is to help youth learn to counterbalance screen time with offline activities. Encourage them to take a digital break and try any offline activity that interests them. Here are some ideas to get you started:

- Visit a park or forest

- Meditate

- Paint

- Create paper crafts

- Make music

- Sing in a choir

- Have a cup of tea

- Talk to someone

Exercise is also a good stress reliever. To keep the ill effects of digital experiences in check, youth should learn to move their bodies every day. Any physical activity that suits their abilities and fitness level will do. Try these:

- Go for a walk

- Group fitness

- Gardening

- Team sports

- Lift weights

- Yoga

- Bike riding / spinning

- House cleaning (!)

Healthy living also benefits from regular unplugged time. Try unplugging at set times each day (teachers can do this in class, too) or have a digital sabbatical one day each week. Longer digital vacations are also a good idea. For more inspiration, check out Christina Crook's work around the joy of missing out (JOMO) at www.experiencejomo.com. Some families choose to partially unplug because they enjoy listening to music or audiobooks, taking photographs, or video chatting with family and friends to share their adventures. While they use technology purposefully in these ways, they also agree not to check email, social media, and blogs. There are lots of ways to approach a digital vacation. Use your discretion on how best to implement it for your family or classroom.

To help youth unplug, support them as they develop a personalized disconnection ritual. Creating a formal transition from online time to offline time can make it easier to log off. A few minutes spent closing apps, clearing remaining notifications, confirming urgent emails have been dealt with, and saying goodnight to online friends can help ease the way from screen time to the next activity. Power down devices or put them in airplane mode to close the disconnection ritual. This is also a good moment to plug in devices so that they are ready for use next time.

Finally, make sure youth understand that "You don't need to post every second of every day to have an impact." That's great advice from Rob Hatch, cofounder of Owner Media Group. A break from social media might be just the thing a youth needs.

Parents will find a blend of physical, emotional, social, and spiritual techniques that work for specific youth. Teachers, similarly, will create a blended approach that support the diverse youth in classrooms. Overall, the goal is the same to create a supportive environment where youth can learn how to use digital skills in ways that will sustain their well-being for a lifetime.

One last thought: Mental wellness is a continuous journey. It takes sustained effort to maintain the balance between good stress and bad stress, between digital and analog. And along the way, we're all going to make mistakes, have bad days, and struggle from time to time. That's real life, online and offline.

Core Skills

In a sense, every skill in this book could fit in this chapter about core skills for living a digital life. However, we're going to start here with some basic skills and then, in subsequent chapters, we'll talk in detail about social skills, study skills, and safety skills that youth must master.

Children and teens have to learn a whole bunch of life skills before they leave home. In fact, many of them are needed to survive high school! Interestingly, most of these skills can be done without any technology but, increasingly, family homes and classrooms are filled with tech that children and teens need to learn in order to succeed. In places, you'll notice information about the parallel offline version of the skill.

Within this book, you won't find the specifics of how to curate a playlist on YouTube or how to link your Fitbit to your tablet. A quick search on YouTube and you'll find excellent how-to tutorials for almost every app and gadget on the market. Instead, I want to highlight the issues and abilities needed to execute digital skills. In some places, I'll also draw your attention to the analog equivalents youth should learn just in case they don't have access to a web browser, app, or device. Patient lessons and ongoing support from parents, guardians, and teachers is part of that process as youth learn how to do these tasks.

1. Reputation Management

While living a digital life, learning to manage reputation is a vital skill. Every youth has to find a blend of things to share without revealing too much or suffering from FOMO (the fear of missing out). Some youth will share nearly nothing while others will share too much. There's a balance point between sharing all of their raw, unedited moments versus publishing a perfectly polished image.

In my earlier book, *Declutter Your Data* (Self-Counsel Press, 2018), I talk about a framework for deciding what to share online: The 3Ps, as in public, personal, and private. Simply put, every person must decide what information about themselves is public and can be readily available online and what is private and stays offline. In between, is the personal; those elements that make a person unique online. Typically, those facts are curated to share the part of your life you want on display. To help youth understand this concept, work with them to fill in the three columns of the 3Ps worksheet as seen in Sample 9. You'll find blank copies to use on the downloadable forms kit.

Of course, managing your online reputation isn't completely in your control. Youth often experience the hardships of this when friends post unflattering pictures, share illicit moments of underage drinking or public displays of affection, or publish quotes out of context. As youth learn to manage their reputation, they must know that they can ask the person to remove the offending post and that social media tools will allow the post to be reported. Of course, youth also learn that once something is online it can be hard to erase it. Another student might screen capture and reshare the item, for example.

Peers are not the only challenge youth face when it comes to reputation management. Parents are also a potential source of embarrassment and angst. Too many publicly posted potty training videos or tantrums or messy bedroom shaming rants can harm a youth's reputation. So, parents and guardians need to look at their own posting behavior and let youth know that they've made mistakes in the past. Express a willingness to delete or hide posts that impact your youth's reputation. Or, take ownership of what you've posted and explain your reasoning to your child. Every family will approach this differently. Ultimately, families may have to comply with legislation.

In her article "When every moment of childhood can be recorded and shared, what happens to childhood?," author Jessica Contrera

Sample 9
The 3Ps

Date: _April 23rd_

Name: _Marie_

Use this worksheet to explore your personal definitions of the 3Ps: what's **public, private, or personal**. These boundaries help youth learn how to manage their reputation online and how to protect their privacy.

Public	Private	Personal
Work history (see LinkedIn) Soccer team news Dad is a city councillor Mom is a notable architect Public events with Mom and Dad	Family stress because of parents' work Grandma has dementia Tried vaping Plantar wart on right foot Scared of thunderstorms Kissed a classmate at the last school dance	Soccer Vacation photos (when home again) Photos with celebrities from public events Shared reading list in GoodReads Post songs on TikTok

notes that, "For the youngest members of the next generation, sometimes called Generation Z, the distinction between the online world and real life is fading." (WashingtonPost.com, December 7, 2016). By extension, I argue, that line between online and real world is blurry for youth today, too.

In 2018, CBC's Ramona Pringle reported on a draft report to find "potential ways to address issues associated with the permanency of personal information online and the effect on reputation." The Office of the Privacy Commissioner of Canada seeks to find ways for youth emerging into adulthood to have control over the content that has been shared about them as children and teens. As Ms. Pringle notes, there is concern that giving individuals carte blanche to "clean up" their digital footprint could lead to essentially "whitewashing" history."

Most importantly, perhaps, she goes on to write, "young people should have the freedom to experiment and explore different aspects of their personalities in their youth without it being held against them once they are adults." (CBC News, 31 Jan 2018). I agree with this wholeheartedly but, at present, youth are seeing the impacts of their online actions. As this fully digital generation grows up, you can help them learn digital life skills so they can avoid making mistakes, and you can be forgiving when mistakes happen.

Fi Birch, Founder of Pro Athlete Online (https://proathlete online.com) helps collegiate and emerging professional athletes to manage their online reputations. She remarked, "The goal of reputation management is to withstand a crisis by building a resilient brand. Crisis prevention is a consideration when posting and, in some cases, removing content but as reputation is the result of perceptions from multiple sources, prevention is not a realistic goal. Because nothing you can do after the fact is as good as what you can do before, you should be creating a digital footprint — right now — that shows the real you. In case there is ever a need for your audience to accept all of you (the good and the bad)." (interview, June 2019).

Reputation management matters because it has impact for future college placements, job opportunities, security clearance, and more. Case in point, "Harvard University has rescinded admissions offers to at least 10 prospective college students after they posted offensive photos and messages on social media." *NBC Boston*, June 4, 2017.

At the same time, an artificially inflated online reputation can have negative consequences, too. For example, "Actress Emma Thompson has said she thinks the trend of movie studios hiring young stars because of their social media following is a 'disaster'." (*The Telegraph*, May 6, 2016.)

In *Declutter Your Data*, I wrote about "posted with permission," an approach to content about children and teens where the youth is consulted before a photo or story is shared online. I still think it's a useful tool for ongoing discussions with youth about reputation management. And it's something that they can use in their own online posts, as well. Yet, posted with permission may not be enough. Taylor Lorenz wrote, "Not all kids react poorly to finding out they've been living an unwitting life online. Some are thrilled." (*The Atlantic*, February 20, 2019). But what about those who aren't thrilled or maybe those who didn't understand the implications of giving permission to post? *The Chicago Tribune* picked up the discussion and Heidi Stevens noted, "A kid may welcome — even crave — internet fame at, say, 9 or 11 or 15. But they may regret some of that exposure as they get older, Heitner said, when they want to forge their own identities without a lot of preconceived notions to combat." (February 26, 2019). Shortly after, this was published: "Gwyneth Paltrow's teenage daughter has criticised her mother for posting a picture of her online without her consent, a reaction experts say will become more common as a generation that has been snapped since their birth grows up." (*The Guardian*, March 29, 2019). It's a complex reputation management choreography and not all the dancers know the steps.

> There is a fine line between sharing parenting experiences and exploiting your kids' life stories.

It's worth discussing that profile pictures generally show a perfect moment in time when someone looks and feels their best with flattering angles and lighting. In contrast, tagged photos often catch people in less flattering moments when their hair is messy or they're sweaty after a workout or they're doing something silly. People cultivate a beautiful version of themselves online but it's not a true representation of their entire being.

2. Time Management

As youth gain autonomy, they are increasingly responsible for their own time management. They learn what time they have to get up in order to get to their first class of the day, hopefully allowing time to eat breakfast, pack a lunch, and attend to at least some personal hygiene. They've also got to manage after-school activities, team training schedules, and homework.

At its simplest, time management is about being alert to the next task at the right moment. Learning to set an alarm to wake up in the morning is a good beginning. Some youth learn to do this with the clock function on their mobile phone while others use an old-school alarm clock on the nightstand. Either is fine — it all depends on a family's approach to technology in the bedroom.

A quick word about watches, clocks, and calendars. Faye Luxemberg-Hyam, a bead-jewelry artisan and retired children's advocate, offered a reminder that it is important that children and teens learn to read an analog clock, not just a digital one. The clock display on many mobile phones can be converted to the clock face, if needed. Similarly, understanding how to read a wall calendar is useful when it comes to scheduling both online and offline.

Activities throughout the day can be managed in a variety of ways. Sometimes the youth takes the lead while other times the parent dictates what's next. Of course, at school, the timetable rules all: students, teachers, and administrators. In my family, each family member is responsible for our own alarms and we each have a Google Calendar. These shared overlapping calendars let us keep track of after-school activities and conflicting parent commitments that need a solution. In contrast, Peggy Richardson's family uses their Google Home assistant to announce reminders, such as when it is time to wake up, leave for school countdown, evening shower reminders, and lights out. And there are families that use analog tools like wall calendars or agenda books. Some even use tools like EasyDaysies™, a magnetic visual schedule invented by Elaine Tan Comeau, with versions for children, youth, and adults (www.easydaysies.com).

Another digital skill is to learn to use the reminder function in your mobile phone. When her children were going on an extended vacation with another family member, Dr. Vanessa Lapointe shared on her Facebook page that she "put the biggest roaming plan possible on my eldest's phone ... and scheduled him a few daily reminders." Each of those reminders was a nudge to send Mom a text and let her know how things were going. In doing so, she modeled a great way for youth to learn to manage their own reminders.

The American Academy of Pediatrics offers a free online calculator for families to help parents figure out how youth will spend time online. I suggest parents build a time management model in cooperation with youth so that they learn to budget the limited amount of time in each day. www.healthychildren.org/English/media/Pages/default.aspx

---

As in all things, each family is unique and what works for one member of the family might be different than what works for another family member. Overall, introduce youth to a variety of methods so that they can understand when information is given to them in that format and so that they can select the tools that work best for them.

3. Privacy

Privacy is a tricky topic. In part, parents and guardians want to ensure that their youth's online world is hidden behind privacy settings, as much as possible. However, youth are also learning to navigate the wider world and, in reality, everything that's online has the potential to be public, no matter the privacy settings.

In general, my approach is to cultivate a culture where youth privacy is respected. If you follow my lead, you'll dive into youth's privacy alongside them as a digital escort. In contrast, other parents want full access to check every account, every post, every file at random. Journalist Marisa Cohen summarized it beautifully in her article "How Much Privacy Do You Give Your Kids?" (*Real Simple*, October 2018) when she wrote, "While the hands-off method works for my family, parents have to decide what makes sense for them. Many of my friends go the opposite way, frequently and unapologetically eyeballing their kids' personal communications."

At the same time, our overarching goal is to teach youth to manage their own privacy. They may use the 3Ps framework noted earlier in this chapter and give it thought in advance. But they'll share things they shouldn't and have their privacy invaded by friends, family, or teachers.

4. Navigation

If you're living a digital life, you've inevitably used Google Maps, or similar, to navigate with the help of GPS. Youth, too, learn to put in a destination and find their way.

If youth are new to digital maps, it can be helpful to show them that there are a variety of route options for walking, bike riding, driving, or taking transit. You can teach them how to alter the route, how to add additional stops in the journey, and how the estimated time of arrival can help them with time management. Whether traveling as a pedestrian, cyclist, private vehicle driver, or transit rider, they'll learn to find their way around town.

However, navigation is one area where many families are prioritizing reading paper maps. Sean Smith, a retired Canadian Army veteran and, today, a training officer with Canadian Air Cadets highlighted the issue when he said, "Situational awareness gets lost when people don't see what's around them." To counteract this, Megan Fox encourages her son to pay attention to his surroundings so that he can get around without relying on a mobile phone. She'll have him take note of where the family's car is parked on a ferry, figure out how to get to his favorite store at the mall, and navigate a hiking trail out and back to practice this skill. Similarly, Eileen Velthuis wants to ensure her kids know how to read a map. They practice getting around without relying on GPS or Google Maps.

As Nora Young remarked on her CBC Radio program, *Spark*, on February 17, 2019, "In her book, *Artificial Unintelligence: How Computers Misunderstand the World*, [Meredith] Broussard argues that we tend to have a bias towards digital solutions—even if they're not necessarily better, or might be worse, than their analog counterparts." As John Alderman and Christine W. Park wrote, "our senses gather the physical information that surrounds us. This information can't be Googled, but we use it all the time." (www.oreilly.com/ideas/returning-to-our-senses, accessed June 2019.)

5. Communication

When it comes to digital life skills, youth need to learn how to communicate through their devices but they also need interpersonal communication skills. Mutual understanding relies on social conventions and, sometimes, today's communication technology creates a mistaken assumption of mutual understanding.

Foundationally, youth need the basics of polite conversation. They need to know how to address people respectfully. And they need to know that their voice is heard. Those basics stem from the lessons they learned as young children — how to say hello and goodbye, how to say thank you and I'm sorry, how to ask questions and answer questions asked of them. Whether answering a landline or answering a cellular call, they've got to "give good phone" as Kim Plumley would joke. It's about the give and take of conversation, the verbal ping pong, in a sense.

Beyond courtesy, youth need to master a number of tools in order to be fully able to communicate today and in the future. These tools include:

- Phone calls

- Text messages

- Video chats

- Video messages

- Audio calls

- Audio messages

- Emails

- Social media posts

- Social media comments

- And more

It's debatable whether youth need to know how to dial a phone that's not connected to the internet. Some say they should learn, just in case that's the only phone available to them while others say why bother? It's old technology. Similar debates rage over whether they should know how to use a payphone or even the concept of placing a collect call. No matter where your family stands on these issues, have them memorize a few key phone numbers. If it helps, fill in the Contacts to Memorize form in Sample 10. It's also on the download kit. Just in case they are away from their own mobile phone and its built-in contacts directory (or, the battery dies).

Sample 10
Contacts to Memorize

Date: _September 16th_

Name: _Anthony_

Jot down the name and phone number of your most important people. Keep a printout of this list in a safe place in case your battery dies or you can't find your phone. Memorize the most important numbers in case you lose this list!

Family

Mom 604-555-4444

Dad 604-555-2222

Mitch 778-555-8888

Friends

Aiden 778-555-6262

Josh 778-555-9696

Nicholas 778-555-3131

School

Office 604-555-5555

Miss Lynch 778-555-7733

Miss Asher 778-555-8844

Activities / Sports / Clubs

Coach Giacomo 604-555-2525

Coach Hustin 778-555-9933

Rec center 604-555-7529 (PLAY)

Other

Work: Pizza Palace 604-555-7878

Of course, youth today are much more likely to send a text than place a phone call. Or they will video chat with friends through Facetime or similar services. To text efficiently, they'll learn to type with their thumbs at a furious pace and they'll get proficient in a new language of abbreviations and emoticons/emojis. For example, IDK means "I don't know" and TTYL means "talk to you later." For a list to reference, see the texting dictionary at the back of the book; it is also available on the downloadable forms kit.

In addition, the language of emojis will become part of their lexicon. Each emoji has a literal meaning — a pig is a pig; or an implied meaning — a smiley face means happy, for example. In addition, there is a second, somewhat hidden, meaning for some emojis. For example, a volcano emoji might mean orgasm. (You'll read more about sexting in Chapter 6.) As such, youth communication often appears akin to hieroglyphics. An emoji glossary is at the back of this book; it is also available on the downloadable forms kit.

While text messages might be youth's preferred mode of communication, they also need to learn how to send and reply to email messages. Teach them to address an email using the to/cc/bcc fields. And be sure to explain the different between carbon copy (CC) and blind carbon copy (BCC). Show them how to input a subject line and where to type the body of their message. They'll also need to know how to attach attachments and understand that some email servers limit the size of the attachments that can be delivered. You might also want to introduce them to read receipts so that they can request a read receipt and know when to send one. And don't forget to show them how to reply or reply all so that email becomes a two-way communication tool.

6. Finances

As youth start to earn their own money, it's a great opportunity to help them learn about spending and saving. This is true if they're given an allowance, too. No matter the source of their income, banks and credit unions offer banking solutions for all ages. By age 12, most financial institutions will grant a youth debit card, with their cosigning parent's permission.

The bank card is the key to online banking and a good opportunity for them to learn to manage their money digitally. Online banking allows youth to make mobile deposits and to transfer funds between accounts. They also get to experience banking fees and, hopefully, earn a little bit of interest each month. Sending and receiving e-transfers can also be practiced. And, perhaps, they have bills to pay: a monthly mobile phone bill, sports team fees, or school hot lunch program.

Fraudulent text messages and emails asking for money arrive in everyone's inbox eventually. As youth start to manage their own money, help them learn how to spot a fake request for a funds transfer or a phony request to confirm their banking details. In part, this is an extension about the earlier lesson on privacy and it's an opportunity to show them how to detect a fake sender. At first, encourage them to bring questionable messages to a trusted adult and then work with them to show how and why the request is fraud.

That bank card also allows them some shopping freedom to buy goods and services with their own money. Of course, as they use their chip and pin or tap their debit card to buy things, they also learn the lessons of budgeting and funds management. A mobile banking app helps them track their account during a spending spree. Of course, some youth won't be ready for digital banking. Instead, they'll first learn to manage their money with bills and coins they can save and spend. Perhaps, a first step towards digital banking is a money management app that lets them track income and expenses.

Online shopping typically requires a credit card. As youth get closer to adulthood, their parent or guardian might entrust them with a supplemental credit card on the adult's account. Other youth wait until they are able to take out a card in their own name. Visa and Master-Card actively promote to young adults to encourage them to take on a credit card.

Credit cards open up another layer of digital money management experiences. Online shopping (and returns) are now quick and easy. Purchasing apps and in-app purchases are also possible. Even younger youth may have access to app purchases through a connected parent's credit card account. In some cases — Starbucks, for example — youth only need a gift card to load value into a mobile purchase app.

Learning to shop online also means learning to interpret product reviews. Youth need to know that it is unethical to leave fake reviews and be encouraged to consider reviews with a critical eye. When looking at online reviews, the following patterns are usually an indication that something isn't right:

- Five-star reviews with very brief comments (if you love a product wouldn't you say lots about why it's so great?)

- Oddly enthusiastic comments about everyday products. No one is that excited about a soap or a pen or a plain white T-shirt in real life.

- Generic statements like "loved it" or "great product" that could be used to review any item.

- Lots of reviews on the same day are suspicious. Legitimate reviews tend to be published at infrequent intervals.

- Lots of reviews on the day the product is released is suspect, too. How can the reviewers have had time to purchase and try the product?

- Overuse of the product name. Legitimate reviews usually mention the brand once, if at all.

- Mentioning competitors' products by brand name is also suspicious review behavior.

- Overuse of synonyms to describe the product. This might be an attempt at latent semantic indexing (LSI), a search engine optimization technique.

- Product photos attached to the reviews that seem familiar. Often a fake reviewer will take many product snapshots in the same place or fake reviewers will share photographs so the same images appear in more than one review.

- If the reviewer isn't a "verified" purchaser then they did not buy the product through that online retailer. Now, it could be they bought it elsewhere, but fake reviews don't usually come from verified buyers.

- How many reviews has the writer provided? Usually, shoppers can click on the reviewer's name to see all their reviews. The number of reviews written and the variety (or lack of variety) in the products reviewed might indicate a fake review account.

To further help online shoppers identify fake reviews, check out these websites:

- Fakespot (www.fakespot.com)

- ReviewMeta (reviewmeta.com)

- Review Summarizer (thereviewindex.com)

Youth will also learn about payments with PayPal, and other online payment systems. They may even set themselves up as a merchant on something like Square to collect money from babysitting, lawn cutting, or other odd jobs.

Finally, youth need to learn about the emerging area of cryptocurrency. Bitcoin and others are available. Using blockchain technology, cryptocurrency is a highly secure, but as yet unregulated global currency.

More than anything, parents and teachers need to help students learn to safeguard their digital money. Accessing online services on protected, not open Wi-Fi networks. Protecting PINs and login passwords. Keeping on top of their spending and alerting a trusted adult if something seems wrong. The goal is to help youth be ready to look after their own money as adults.

7. Streaming

Youth spending time online is often about accessing streaming services. Whether they want the latest TV shows on Netflix or seek a playlist on Spotify, they're accessing streamed, often paid content. Often, families will have an account for these services paid for by parents or guardians. If not, youth may choose to spend their own money to get to the movies, TV shows, and music they want. Or they'll limit themselves to the free streaming content they can find on YouTube and elsewhere online.

To teach youth about streaming, they need skills to understand it in two parts: the technology and the content.

The technology is relatively user friendly. Within a web browser or app they can access content using a simple log-in and password. They don't really need to understand the technology behind the streaming. Youth know it works and how to drive it. For video content they might be using:

- Netflix

- Hulu

- Amazon Prime

- Crave

- Gem

- HBO

- CBS

- YouTube

- Vimeo

- TikTok

- Facebook Watch

Similarly, to find music, there are numerous services available. The most popular ones are:

- Spotify

- Apple Music

- Google Play Music

- Amazon Music

- SiriusXM

As for the content, teachers, parents, and guardians assess what youth will watch up to a certain age. That age will differ depending on the maturity and responsibility demonstrated by specific young people. Their own experience — sheltered or unsheltered — and their experience of trauma and how sensitive they are also influence what they should be allowed to watch. Of course, youth may circumvent adult guidance of any sort. To help them navigate solo, introduce them to the ratings systems.

In the United States, there are different rating systems for movies and television. Canada, United Kingdom, and other countries have similar ratings systems and often repeat the USA classifications. For movies, the ratings are provided by the Classification & Ratings Administration (CARA) as follows:

- G: Suitable for general audiences of all ages.

- PG: Parental guidance recommended for younger viewers.

- PG-13: Stronger parental guidance recommended.

- R: Restricted due to graphic violence, adult situations, or graphic language.

- NC-17: No children under 17 admitted even with a parent or guardian.

To learn more about movie ratings visit https://filmratings.com.

In turn, television shows are rated with children and teens in mind. Here are the television rating categories:

- TV-Y: Suitable for children of all ages.

- TV-Y7: Suitable for children age 7 and older.

- TV-PG: Parental guidance suggested.

- TV-14: Parental guidance strongly suggested. Content unsuitable for youth under 14.

- TV-MA: Suitable for mature audiences.

These television ratings can be further modified by the following descriptor:

- D: Suggestive dialogue

- L: Coarse language

- S: Sexual content

- V: Violence

- FV: Fantasy violence

To learn more about television ratings, visit www.tvguidelines.org.

While ratings are helpful, many streaming viewers disregard them or simply don't look for the information. If you're entrusting youth to monitor their own streaming habits, you can use these frameworks to agree on what's appropriate viewing.

8. Around the House

We are living during the rise of the "Internet of Things" or IoT. As more and more homes adopt internet-connected devices, youth need to know how to operate these devices for their safety and the comfort of their family.

Typically, they first learn to use them so that they can secure the house when they leave and enter the house when they return. This might involve passwords or proximity keys built into their smartphones that grant access to the main part of the house and any outbuildings such as a garage or tool shed. They might also be able to monitor security cameras outside the home or know that they are under surveillance inside the home.

Of course, once they get home from school and on weekends, youth typically contribute to household chores that need to be done. They may do their own laundry, vacuum the floors, or cook a meal.

In the kitchen, making a snack or meal might involve getting food from a smart fridge or cooking on a programmable stove. They may choose to weigh their food with a smart scale and track calorie intake with a fitness app. A verbal command to Alexa or Siri might allow the youth to add to the family grocery shopping list. (And, yes, many families still use a notepad and pen on the counter.)

And then there's meal preparation. A little bit of chef in training support can help youth thrive in the kitchen. Over time, teach them the basics of boiling water (high-tech kettles!) and making toast (toasters don't just toast anymore). Then add in small appliances like the InstantPot or stand mixer. As youth learn their way around the kitchen, they may need guidance to find reliable recipes online or in cookbooks (ebook format, perhaps?). And they'll need to know how to convert units (another app or a small math calculation) to convert liters to gallons, Celsius to Fahrenheit, and kilograms to pounds. Empower youth to be able to prepare some meals and snacks on their own.

As I was writing this book, Chef Nathan Hyam reminded me that one of the skills youth might miss out on is a connection to food. With grocery delivery and take-out food so readily available, youth might not know how to grow food or, even, how to identify food in its original form. Your family might choose to introduce youth to the tactile realities of gardening and farming. Help them learn the difference between plants and weeds. Foster an appreciation for all the work that goes into growing food. Teach them when food is ready to harvest and how to preserve it. It's another opportunity to encourage offline time as part of the mental wellness goals for all digital citizens.

In the laundry room, it may feel like you need a degree in physics to run the washer and dryer. Heck, my high efficiency washing machine's motor sounds like an airplane landing in my laundry room sometimes! Youth need guidance to understand the various settings so they can run a load of clothes through the wash/dry cycle.

The laundry room might also be where youth could pause to do some simple sewing such as attaching a button or fixing a hem. Even if they use needle and thread to make the repair, they might need to place an online order for thread, zippers, buttons, or other sewing notions to get the job done. To shop online they've got to know the name of the notion they need — bobbins, eyelets, seam ripper, and more.

General housekeeping also has digital elements. Vacuuming and dusting might require a programmable gadget (Roomba!). Even cleaning the bathroom might require some technological skill if you invested in a toilet cleaning robot.

Temperature control throughout the house may also be digitally driven. My niece called me because her family's new house was so cold; it turned out she didn't know how to turn on the heat. Heated floors are also a learning curve that come with electricity use expenses. Smart fans, programmable furnaces, air conditioning units, and more all require some digital skills these days.

Add to all that smart assistants like Alexa and Siri that can listen to our commands to play music, order groceries, and more. Today's youth are growing up in a very different world, if your family embraces the internet of things.

You'll notice that throughout this section, I've mentioned some analog alternatives. Not every family is ready to embrace the IoT. Some are overwhelmed by all the new technology to learn (and the expense!) while others are making a conscious choice to not use IoT. That choice is driven by privacy and security concerns. Is your home secure if your smart lock can be hacked? What privacy do you give up if your smart TV or smart speaker is listening to your family's life every day? Of course, in some cases, the convenience of some IoT technology (e.g., app-driven lightbulbs) overrides concerns about any risks. As with all things digital, every family will pick IoT devices that suit their needs, wants, and budget.

9. Physical Fitness

One of the hallmarks of healthy digital living is achieving a balance between online activities and real world movement. With some irony, I write this to affirm that digital living can both help and hinder our physical fitness efforts.

As Sue Palmer wrote, "Today's children have far fewer opportunities for what I call 'real play'. They are no longer learning through first-hand experiences how to be human and are much less likely to play or socialise outdoors or with others." (*The Daily Mail*, January 27, 2016.) If children are playing less, this helps define youth, too.

And you read in Chapter 2 about the impacts screen time has on sleep (blue light, etc.).

Yet, Dr. Kendall Ho, a researcher at the University of British Columbia, shared a hopeful view for fitness technology at the Innovation Forum in Maple Ridge (April 2, 2019). Dr. Ho shared that he regularly prescribes diet and exercise apps and wearable technology to his patients to support them in their health journeys. In fact, Dr. Ho sees "edibles as the next wearables" as business and medicine collaborate on technology solutions for patients. Imagine swallowing a pill-sized bot (the edible) capable of scanning your digestive tract and sending medical data to your doctor via Bluetooth. An app, wearable, or edible might help a diabetic patient track blood sugar and insulin. Another might help a concussion patient monitor their heart rate as they return to exercise. A third app might help someone struggling to maintain their weight at a healthy level. Depending on youth's medical needs, they might need support to learn and maintain their health with the help of technology.

In addition, I was glad to see Dr. Ho recognize the ethical issues with digital medicine; privacy, confidentiality, fragmentation of care, and access. If you teach youth to use any of these devices then you must also teach them about privacy, confidentiality, and other issues we've discussed elsewhere in this book.

Social Skills

If there's one way youth are using technology, it's social. Tweens and teens are texting, snapping, and messaging their social connections. And this is a great thing! As youth gain independence, they form attachments to people outside their family. It's all part of growing up. That said, the journey from the playground friendships of childhood to the mature friendships of adulthood can be a bumpy ride.

Even before technology was part of the mix, being a teenager was hard. Misunderstandings, miscommunication, and flat-out mistakes happen to everyone as they learn to express themselves and interact with others. Add to that the hormones and new territory of dating and it gets even more complex. Plus, the pool of potential friends gets bigger and bigger as children move to middle school then high school. There's a lot to cope with and a large potential audience that seems to watch each youth as they figure it all out.

Today, technology adds another layer to the experience. Youth learn the mechanics of communication tools and they learn the extra skills needed to build and sustain friendships in a digital environment. They also learn, usually the hard way, that words and emojis can be easily misunderstood and can create hurt feelings, jealousy, and, sometimes, anger-fueled fights. So it's important to help youth learn social skills to live a digital life.

1. Setting up Accounts

To begin, every account needs to be set up. Usually, this is a simple process requiring just a username and password. However, many services have age restrictions. Snapchat, TikTok, Facebook, YouTube, and Instagram all require users to be at least 13 years old. Meanwhile, WhatsApp, LinkedIn, and other tools set the minimum age at 16 years old. However, younger users can easily circumvent these restrictions by lying about their birthdate. These tools have no mechanism to check the accuracy of the birth date provided.

As with all things digital, each youth is unique and the adults closest to them will know if they are ready for a particular social media channel. And, those same adults have to accept that youth will disregard any parental or school restrictions and set up accounts anyway. Challenging authority in this way is all part of growing up.

Assuming an account is being set up, talk to youth about whether to use their real name or a pseudonym. Some social media platforms, including Facebook, require you to use your real name. For security reasons and to protect their digital footprint in future job searches, accounts are often setup using a first name and middle name. Others will use a nickname, e.g., Jon for Jonathan or Jas for Jaspreet. Yet, students looking to get a jump start on their careers will create LinkedIn profiles using their real names.

Further, it's important to note that real names, pseudonyms, or nicknames are only half the battle when it comes to online names. Many social media platforms have a username function: the more visible @name that appears in newsfeeds and chats. The username can be the same as your real name without any spaces or it can be another name altogether. It doesn't even have to be a name; often a fantasy name, initials, or some other handle is selected.

In addition, the username will be unique with only one person using that name on any given platform. For example, last time I checked there were more than 40 people on Instagram who share my real name, Angela Crocker. Yet, I am the only one who can use the @AngelaCrocker username. The other Angela Crockers each have a unique variation on the name behind the @.

Oftentimes, a username represents an alter ego or online persona. This is another way that youth (and adults) can conceal their real identity somewhat. However, it's also a way to create an online presence that gives youth a false sense of anonymity. Hidden beneath their virtual mask, they may be emboldened to do the things they wouldn't regularly do online. It's worthwhile for parents and teachers to reinforce the importance of protecting online identity, even when wearing a digital costume.

2. Passwords

In addition to the username, every account requires a password. It is important to teach youth to develop strong passwords and secure methods of keeping track of them.

As a first step, offer youth the following advice when it comes to creating strong passwords:

- Make every password unique.

- Include both upper and lower case letters.

- Include one or more numbers.

- Include one or more special characters such as *, &, %, $, and #.

- Don't use easy to guess passwords such as "password" or "12345678" or "qwerty."

- Don't use birth dates, address numbers, or other notable personal numbers.

- Never use the same password for more than one account.

In addition, show youth the password strength calculator built into many online accounts. As you create a new password it will be graded on a scale from weak to strong. Aim for a strong password every time. And be sure to change it often, at least quarterly, to reduce the risk of a breach. This could be a reminder on the family calendar for all family members every three months (or whatever interval works for your family.)

As youth grow their online presence, there is an increasing number of account passwords to track. Every family will approach this differently but I encourage parents or guardians to have access to youth's passwords. Some parents will use this information to log in and check what a youth is doing online. Others will keep them for emergency use only — say if the youth is missing or, more likely, their phone has been lost somewhere. As you make these decisions, you'll also want to decide whether to store each youth's passwords separately or as part of a larger family password record.

Tracking passwords is a big job that only gets bigger as more people in a family or classroom have online access to more and more tools. At school, a student might have a password to access the school's computers, another to access the music lab computers, and a third to log into Office 365. With 30 students in a typical classroom, that's up to 90 passwords per class. At the middle school and high school levels, a teacher might see 5 or more classes each day. Suddenly, that's 450 passwords — yikes! Of course, forgotten passwords can be reset if needed but that takes time away from the lesson. Instead, teachers encourage students to memorize and document their passwords for school.

At home, each family member will have many accounts so it's a good idea to have a centralized password system. An egalitarian approach is to have every family member, parents included, put their passwords in a safe location with the understanding that the passwords will not be used without consent unless there is an emergency. That way, any family member can access a forgotten password, if needed. Alternatively, a family could go a step further and have a spreadsheet stored in the cloud (Dropbox, iCloud, OneDrive, Google Drive). The spreadsheet would include the service, username, and password. Have a look at Sample 11 and then build your own Online Account Inventory using the template available in the download kit.

If your family prefers an analog approach, try putting password details in sealed envelopes, in a notebook, or in a file folder. Pencil on paper solutions are functional but be alert that paper can go missing and is susceptible to spilled drinks, shredding accidents, and other mishaps. The hard part, usually, is remembering to update these handwritten notes when passwords are updated.

Your digital approach might include a spreadsheet such as the one shown in Sample 11 or your family might try a password manager service. However, it's important to note that cloud storage services can be breached so there's some risk that the information will be stolen. That said, this method is one that feels comfortable and familiar to many families and it's often used.

Another digital option is to use a password manager or password wallet through services like 1password (www.1password.com), Dashlane (www.dashlane.com), KeePassX (www.keepassx.org), and LastPass (www.lastpass.com). Depending on the level of service you need, the

Sample 11
Online Account Inventory

Date: _November 18th_

Name: _Patricia_

Use this worksheet to create a list of all your online accounts with the logins and password information. Be sure to keep this document in a safe place to protect your digital footprint. You can create one master list for the whole family or generate a unique list for each person.

Account	Login	Password	Notes
TikTok	pat@email.com	24;fl1ght	
Instagram	pat@email.com	P1ane)(73	
Email	server@email.com	87aNg31;	
Dropbox	patricia@sD99.ca	Hawks:256	for school
Office 365	patricia@sD99.ca	haWks:652	for school
Mobile phone	n/a	3232	also thumbprint

costs range from free to about $5 USD per month. Some, including LastPass, offer a family account where the passwords of up to six family members can be managed within a password wallet. These services track all your passwords and your only responsibility is to remember a single master password that gives you access to all accounts. These services are advantageous from a security point of view because they generate long and complex passwords. Of course, some users don't feel comfortable putting so much trust in one service.

No matter how you choose to store your passwords, the key lesson is to ensure youth understand how to create a strong password, the importance of protecting each password, and methods to document passwords securely.

3. Family Relationships

Whether your family is related by blood, by marriage, or by choice, technology has the power to bring families closer together. Imagine a grandparent attending a graduation ceremony through livestreaming, or a geographically distant aunt enjoying a weekly video chat. Technology allows you to include people who are far away in those special occasions and everyday moments.

Show youth how to join family conversations online. If they are ready for these apps, they might join conversations in myriad apps including:

- Facetime, Skype, Zoom, or other video chats
- Group text messages in plain text or using WhatsApp, Messenger, or other tools
- Two-way "walkie talkie" style video chats with singles or groups in Marco Polo
- Email conversations using "reply all"

Technology can be helpful to fostering family relationships. When I travel on business, nightly video chats with my son and husband keep us connected. It's comforting to see one another and interact in real time. Author Mike Brooks, PhD, co-author of *Tech Generation: Raising Balanced Kids in a Hyper-Connected World*, (Oxford University Press, 2018) was quoted in the March 2019 edition of *Real Simple* magazine. He shared that each member of his family curates a Spotify playlist that the family listens to together while doing other activities. He noted, "The trick is use the technology to create a shared experience that increases bonding, rather than isolating us." My family does something similar as we continue our road trip tradition of listening to audiobooks while on holiday. To date, we've enjoyed the work of Michael Bond, Eoin Colfer, Terry Pratchett, and Meg Cabot. Whether we're enjoying the adventures of Paddington or Artemis Fowl or vicariously traveling to Discworld or Genovia, we share the experience.

When all family members can be together in person, create a collective agreement about whether technology is allowed and where. Some families will say no technology in the bedrooms or, maybe, no phones at the dining table. Others will have a rule that no one watches videos or plays games alone. In addition, other families, including mine, will enjoy screen time "alone, together." By this I mean we sit companionably in the same room while each enjoying our own screen activities. While I stream the latest episode of my favorite television show, my husband might read an ebook, and our son plays a game on his iPad.

Every family will approach this differently but the key is to find ways to have technology nurture shared experiences when it makes sense rather than allowing them to isolate family members in separate rooms alone and likely lonely.

4. Being a Good Friend

Online friendships can be awkward. When kids and teens are just learning how to build and maintain friendships, the digital element can make it extra challenging. Yet, "socially isolated kids can find one another online in communities of shared interest. They can make connections that might be more difficult if attempted in person. The asynchronous and performative nature of social media can give kids more time to present themselves without awkwardness, and this can be a huge confidence boom to kids who may struggle to fit in with peers." (Devorah Heitner, PhD, *Screenwise: Helping Kids Thrive (and Survive) in Their Digital World*, Bibliomotion Inc., 2016). Partly, youth are going to figure out social connections through trial and error. But, parents and teachers can offer some guidance along the way.

Encourage youth to use technology to build and sustain friendships, in addition to their face-to-face time together. Adding an audio (or video) chat with a tool like Discord creates opportunities for negotiation, collaboration, and just plain fun when playing games like *Terraria* or *Roblox*. A group chat on WhatsApp, Facebook Messenger, or the like can accomplish the same thing but the two-way conversation of audio or video chat has a real-time social element.

If they are communicating by text message, let's show youth how text-only conversations lack the social cues that come with facial expression and tone of voice. When they're absent, these things influence the meaning of your words. The experience of an in-person or video chat with visual clues is really different than a text message alone.

Youth can also learn ways to send more personal messages to specific people. Personalized one-on-one communication can be a good way to keep a friendship real. For example, text messaging software allows youth to send a 60-second voice message. Youth can also send private thoughts through text or direct message (DM). Send a video reply in Facebook Messenger or WhatsApp. Share links that amuse you or might interest your friend. Youth can even learn to set-up a recurring appointment for a video chat or voice call. This can be especially helpful if a family has relocated to a new city and old friends are now far away. By sending personalized messages to specific people, youth learn to foster true friendships.

Even if separated by distance, youth can watch the same streaming movie at the same time and simultaneously chat through text, audio, or video emulating the interaction they would share if they were in the same room.

There's also a place for youth to learn how to send snail mail. A card or letter in a friend's mailbox can be a fun surprise. And there's a parallel lesson in managing your contacts to keep track of mailing addresses. Or just pop that note into the ventilation slot in your friend's locker at school. Same effect without the cost of a stamp.

While Eric Andrew-Gee wrote, "[smartphones] are making us worse at being alone and worse at being together." ("Your Smartphone is Making You Stupid," *The Globe & Mail*, April 10, 2018). Youth are going to continue to communicate through technology so let's give them some skills that reduce the loneliness and increase the connection.

5. School, Parties, and Social Events

When it comes to in-person events, technology is both a help and a hindrance. "Technology that is so social, so geared towards being in touch constantly, is also very disruptive to our in-person social contact. On-line closeness comes at the expense of offline closeness," says Mariek Vanden Abeele, PhD, a professor of information and communication science at Tilburg University in the Netherlands. (Thrive Global, October 19, 2018). Yet, events are constantly being organized online.

Youth are learning to navigate the social scene in a world filled with technology. On a practical level, they learn how to organize events online. Whether they use text messages, a Facebook event, or something like Eventbrite, the basics of who should be where and when can be organized digitally.

What's problematic is when an in-person event is happening. Some social settings allow for youth to use their phones. They might be taking pictures, sharing videos, making videos, or showing each other tech tricks. Yet, this behavior can be seen as rude and antisocial, even an unhealthy attachment to a phone. And sometimes it is!

The ability to connect with people in real life (IRL) is a skill learned over a lifetime. Making conversation with relative strangers of all ages is a daunting task. And youth accustomed to communicating through their phones may find it even more difficult. As with all digital life skills, youth have to learn to entertain themselves without technology in groups (and when they're alone).

Youth need guidance to understand that using a mobile phone to connect online while in the presence of a friend (IRL) sends a signal that the person in the same room is less important than the person online. This can result in a feeling of social rejection, something that's definitely damaging to a relationship. Helping youth understand this impact may help them alter their behavior. And one of the best ways for that to happen is to have adults model the behavior. We can't reasonably expect youth to disconnect if the adults around them are constantly checking email or social feeds during in person events.

6. Notifications and Distractions

As an experiment, ask the youth in your life to track their notifications over a period of time. This can be done individually, as a family, or with an entire class. A teacher conducted this experiment with her students. In just 30 minutes her 23 students received 268 notifications from text messages, social media, and other alerts. In her viral Facebook post summarizing this experiment, she pleaded with parents to stop students from bringing phones to class. (The post has since been deleted so I share this story anonymously to protect the teacher's identity.)

I would argue that parents, teachers, and school administrators can work in collaboration to set boundaries around mobile phones in class as they do serve as learning technology in many classrooms. Setting boundaries in controlled environments is only half the battle. To function in the wider world, youth need to learn and understand the impacts of notifications and the beeps, buzzes, and bings that come with them. Not only are they distracting to the youth who owns the phone but they are distracting to everyone around them.

Distraction of any sort reduces productivity. Every time a person is distracted they lose their place and it can take minutes to return to the task they were trying to accomplish. And distractions are an epidemic in the era of smartphones. Parents and teachers can help youth learn to minimize distractions in many ways including:

- Turning phones to silent.

- Turning off phone vibrations.

- Denying apps the opportunity to send notifications.

- Selecting only specific notifications within an app. For example, allowing notifications for direct messages but turning off the ones for likes and comments.

- Using the VIP or important contact function in your contacts app so that notifications from only a select group of people will come through.

- Using Do Not Disturb settings during set times (e.g., school hours or overnight)

- Installing an app like Let Me Sleep that turns off all noises from the phone during a set period of time.

In combination, these techniques will minimize the number of notifications and reduce the number of distractions. Of course, minimizing notifications also means that youth need to get in the habit of checking for messages regularly.

7. Gaming

Not all youth love gaming online but those who do will immerse themselves in that virtual world. Whether they play *Fortnite*, *Minecraft*, *Candy Crush*, or any other game, youth can be intensely engaged by these games.

For parents and teachers that commitment to a game can be positive or negative. On the plus side, games often involve problem solving, cooperation, and entertainment. On the downside, games can be all-consuming, potentially addictive, and the suspected source of many problems. Parents and teachers also have to distinguish between the ill effects of a video game or gaming disorder from the back talk from a sassy teenager testing their boundaries.

Youth who are interested in gaming need guidance to ensure that they balance their online time with healthy living activities as we talked about in Chapter 2. If they are performing well at school, getting regular physical activity, eating (at least some) nutritious food, and looking after their personal hygiene, then any remaining time devoted to gaming seems reasonable. For those youth that are missing out on the healthy living standards in order to make more time for gaming, then there's an unhealthy imbalance. In some cases, they won't be able to control when they start or stop playing a game nor control how long they'll play.

The World Health Organization (WHO) added "gaming disorder" to its classification of diseases in late 2017. As Eddie Makuch wrote, "People suffering from the so-called 'gaming disorder' run the risk of 'significant impairment' to their personal, family, social, education, and occupational lives, according to the WHO. The description goes on to say that gaming disorder can be a continuous condition or it can be episodic or recurrent in nature." (Gamespot.com, January 2, 2018). When youth are suffering the impacts of gaming activity, adult intervention is needed.

In contrast, some research related to gaming and found the results to be less worrying. Peter Gray, PhD, reported on the work of gaming researchers Patrick Markey and Christopher Ferguson who found that "video gaming raises dopamine levels in the brain to about the same degree that eating a slice of pepperoni pizza or dish of ice cream does (without the calories). That is, it raises dopamine to roughly double its normal resting level, whereas drugs like heroin, cocaine, or amphetamine raise dopamine by roughly ten times that much." (*Psychology Today*, March 2018.) Dr Gray's report went on to note that "neuroscientist Marc Palaus and his colleagues (2017) published a systematic review of all the research they could find—derived from a total of 116 published articles — concerning effects of video gaming on the brain. The results are what anyone familiar with brain research would expect. Games that involve visual acuity and attention activate parts of the brain that underlie visual acuity and attention. Games that involve spatial memory activate parts of the brain involved in spatial memory." Bottom line? "Yes, video gaming can alter the brain, but the documented effects are positive, not negative." (*Psychology Today*, March 2018.)

No matter the clinical analysis, youth are playing games with enthusiasm. So, what digital life skills do they need to navigate them effectively?

First, you can introduce them to the game ratings. Similar to the ratings given to film and television, the gaming industry also has a rating system established by the Entertainment Software Rating Board (ESRB). "Its rating system works in three parts: a rating category that describes the overall age appropriateness of the product, a content descriptor, and a warning if the game has elements allowing interactions with other players (which, obviously, cannot be rated). The content ratings are 'C' or 'EC' (Early Childhood), 'E' (Everyone), 'E10+' (Everyone over the age of 10), 'T' (Teen), 'M' (Mature), 'A' or 'AO' (Adults only), and 'RP' (Rating Pending). There are currently 30 descriptors and three warnings about interactions, as well. " (https://www.hg.org/legal-articles/how-do-movies-tv-shows-music-and-video-games-get-rated-for-content-35246, accessed July, 2019).

Next, youth need to be aware of the potential costs within games. In-app and in-game purchases may extend the play value or add new features. Game specific currency is also available for purchase with real dollars, a revenue stream worth billions of dollars to the gaming industry. While they may want to make those purchases, families will have to decide how to deal with game expenses. Some will allow youth to spend freely without restrictions. Others will only allow parent-authorized purchases. Another approach is to allow the youth to spend their own money on game currency; something my son does without a credit card by purchasing gift cards for his favorite online games at the local video game store. All in all, it's a financial lesson about budgeting income and expenses.

On another front, be sure your youth knows how to file a report within a game. If they encounter a troll or have some sort of in-game glitch, being able to report it in real time increases the likelihood that they'll recover their loss, if any.

8. Influence and Influencers

Youth are heavily influenced by their peers both online and offline. As parents and teachers, you have to teach them the impact of influence: impact on their well-being and mental health as well as impact on their thoughts and actions.

Influencers sway the opinions and buying decisions of their audience. That audience is a combination of fans and followers across social media, email newsletters, podcasts, blogs, flash briefings, and any other digital platforms they use. There are four broad categories of influencer based on the size of their audiences including:

- Celebrity influencers who have a massive audience of millions of people.

- Macro influencers who have a large audience of tens of thousands, possibly hundreds of thousands of people.

- Micro influencers who have a modest audience of a 1,000 to 10,000 people.

- Nano influencers who have a relatively small audience under a 1,000 people.

Those Nano influencers include the friends and classmates youth connect with through social media. Influence can be both positive and negative. As Jean M. Twenge, PhD, noted "many people post only their successes online, so many teens don't realize that their friends fail at things, too. The social media profiles they see make them feel like failures. If they spent more time with their friends in person, they might realize that they are not the only ones making mistakes." (*iGen: Why Today's Super-Connected Kids Are Growing Up Less Rebellious, More Tolerant, Less Happy — and Completely Unprepared for Adulthood*, Atria Paperback, 2017). As youth mature to adulthood, they learn this truth.

Youth need to learn to be alert to the impact influencers can have on them. As they learn to navigate the digital world, they also learn to resist or accept the influences around them both online and offline.

9. Content Creation and Curation

As youth grow their social skills online, they learn to share content. Photos, links, videos, writing, and more can all be shared with friends and family, teachers, and classmates. In broad terms, there are two types of content: created and curated. Created content is original content made by the youth. It's the photos they've taken, the words they've written, and their original videos. In parallel, youth also curate existing content produced by others. They learn to share their favorite music, funny pictures, interesting links, and more.

One of my earlier books, *The Content Planner* (Self-Counsel Press, 2017), introduces readers to the content-planning cycle. This nine-step approach helps individuals and businesses determine what content they want to create, why they're going to create it, who will consume the content, and where it will be published. Youth who are keenly interested in establishing a video channel, podcast, or blog may find this approach a helpful guide.

Youth have an ad hoc approach to content creation and curation. Initially, their reasons for sharing content will be purely for fun and, over time, they'll likely incorporate some educational content, too. Their audience, most often, will be their peers and, possibly, family members or teachers. As for where they'll publish, most likely they'll choose one or more social media platforms.

Content creation itself is a whole series of interrelated digital skills. These include:

- Writing copy
- Spell check and grammar check
- Document formatting
- Taking photos and video
- Editing photos and video
- Making memes
- Recording audio
- Tagging

Depending on their content interests, all of these tasks can be done with a computer, tablet, or mobile phone. You'll read more about the specifics in Chapter 5 on Study Skills.

10. Social Media

In general, both positive and negative benefits are baked into social media. On the positive side, youth learn to communicate through digital tools; they connect with friends, find their community online (and off), and develop a freer sense of self expression. In contrast, these same youth are struggling under immense social pressure to curate their online image, learning the social codes of online living for their age group, and facing mental health issues aggravated by excessive time on screens, interrupted sleep, detached family relationships, and more. Parents and teachers can provide support to help youth find the positive and productive uses of social media while minimizing the negative and unwelcome aspects.

Rather than ban social media altogether, I recommend that parents and teachers find incremental ways to scaffold social media skills in youth. By this, I mean, start them off slowly and help them learn how to use the tools to positive effect while also being alert to the pitfalls including loss of sleep, social stress, and mental illness including anxiety and depression. (For more on wellness, review Chapter 2.)

As youth explore social media, they should take on just one platform at a time. Suddenly navigating Snapchat, Instagram, and TikTok all at the same time is a cognitive overload that their minds (and their adult mentors' minds!) won't be able to process. Instead, advise them to start with one platform and add others only when the first has been mastered. And know that they might disregard your advice and start up accounts without your knowledge.

Social media mastery is a two-fold process. In part, it's the technical functioning of the platform itself. Setting up an account is part of this. Learning how the app works is the larger lesson; from connecting with friends and strangers to sharing content to understanding location and privacy settings. But once the mechanics are organized, the second-part of the two-fold process comes into play. These lessons have to do with content sharing, engagement, time management, and social impacts. In a sense, it's about learning how to live with the social network in a healthy way within the context of real life.

The youth we focus on in this book range in age from 11 to 18. All of these users are continually observing social interactions online and in person. They are exploring and practicing how to interact one-on-one, within groups, and between groups. Younger users in this age range will be learning how to build and maintain friendships. As they age, they'll join their older peers as they begin dating and exploring sexual relationships.

The use of social media can be a particular problem for educators as students conduct parts of their school relationships online. Unkind words, digital arguments, and/or bullying language can spill over into classroom interactions. Social ingroups and outgroups play out in group projects, class assignments, and in the hallways. It's a challenging setting for teachers and administrators. This is one of the major reasons parents, guardians, teachers, and school administrators have to work together to create community standards about mobile phone use at school and to mitigate the impacts of social media on learning environments.

Schools play an important role in that ongoing dialogue. Online communication, and social media, in particular, can and should be addressed in a variety of lessons from health education to computers to citizenship courses. Curriculum across several disciplines can open up discussion about social media and keep students talking about the opportunities and issues.

In addition, schools are being increasingly proactive about bringing in guest speakers to talk to both students and parents, together and separately. Near my home, as a parent, I've observed educational talks from Jessie Miller (www.mediatedreality.com), Brandon Laur (www. thewhitehatter.ca), and Nick Chernoff (saferschoolstogether.com). There are similar experts in every major city and schools are tapping this expertise as a much needed resource.

I am available to conduct workshops for parents, teachers, and students on digital life skills for youth and related topics such as digital decluttering, online community building, and content planning. For more information, visit angelacrocker.com/school-visits.

While teachers present relevant curriculum and schools bolster the discussions with additional resources for students and parents, this is only part of the ongoing solution. Parents and guardians must be involved in their students' social media lives. As with so many aspects of digital living, this includes modeling best practices, observing social media accounts, auditing mobile phone usage, and more. Sadly, many youth are not mentored or monitored in any way and this often leads to the difficulties schools have to navigate.

Collectively, parents, teachers, and guardians want to reinforce the longevity of each person's digital footprint. In short: What goes on the internet stays on the internet. Even deleted posts, comments, photos, and files can be recovered. The internet never forgets and we have to reinforce this fact for youth repeatedly as they learn to manage their digital footprint, especially through social media.

So, what actions can youth take to manage their digital footprint? The first lessons should be about general guidelines that apply to all social media platforms. These include:

- Pick and choose what social media to use. You don't have to use it all.

- Use age-appropriate social media sites. For example, Instagram is for users age 13 and above.

- Be human. You are a person talking to other people.

- Think before you post. Ask yourself: Is it true? Is it kind? Is it necessary?

- Make sure the post is appropriate; especially, no nudity or foul language.

- Take the face-to-face test. Would you make the same comment to the person if you saw them?

- Take the headline test. Would you feel good if your post was the headline on a newspaper's front page tomorrow?

- Check your privacy settings. Don't assume the default settings are all you need. And re-check them each time the app updates.

- Know that private isn't always private. Friends can screen-capture and share "friends-only" posts publicly.

- Remember that you can't know who's behind the screen name. It may look like a friend but it might be a stranger.

- Understand gamification. Know that social media platforms are designed to make you stay on longer and check in more often.

- Understand vanity metrics. The number of likes, comments, and followers don't validate your worth. Instead, learn to value meaningful metrics: engagement, conversations, education, entertainment.

During a 2018 appearance in Vancouver, former First Lady Michelle Obama had this to say: "Social media can do two things: it can bring us together or keep us isolated. " ("Michelle Obama talks social media and raising daughters at Vancouver event," CBC News, February 15, 2018). If isolation and loneliness are at the root of anxiety and depression, then youth have to learn ways to use social media that bring us together. Author, parent, and digital expert Alexandra Samuel said it well on CBC Radio's *The Current*, "I think it's far more useful to ask yourself how this incredibly powerful medium can actually support you in your own personal goals" (December 9, 2016). I agree wholeheartedly. Let's show youth how it can support their goals.

Of course, what adults think about social media doesn't always resonate with youth. Each demographic trends to using different social media tools in different ways. "I think Facebook is more for old people and, like, adults. My parents use Facebook. I honestly have never been on Facebook. " Noah Schapp, then age 13, costar of the Netflix series *Stranger Things* (*Adweek*, October 30, 2017).

Add to that the varied experience of adults — some love social media, and others hate it. Some have embraced it and then walked away completely while others continue to use it as a necessary communication channel for work and/or leisure. Your opinion might influence the youth in your life. In some cases it will spark them to want to try social media and in other cases it may put them off the whole idea.

Assuming youth in your life are exploring social media, here 's a quick overview of the most popular social media channels today.

10.1 Snapchat

Snapchat is a photo and short video sharing social network. Photos and videos can be shared with all followers or with a subset of friends or even a single person. Each photo shared is a "snap." The photos and videos shared disappear when viewed and are deleted after 24 hours if they are not viewed. The content is temporary. If a screen capture is taken, Snapchat sends a notice to the person who posted the content to let them know who took the screen capture and puts a record in the chat log.

Adults take note: Snapchat has a built-in "My Eyes Only" folder where images can be saved in a hidden folder. Enter the wrong password and the folder's contents are instantly deleted. Youth often use this folder to conceal illicit images.

Snap streaks — the in-app gamification that keeps users participating daily — is one unhealthy function of Snapchat. Youth who focus solely on maintaining Snap streaks lose the social connection in favor of simply maintaining the streak.

Given the disappearing nature of Snapchat content, this platform is used by youth for sexting (sexually explicit text messages) and sharing nude photographs. You'll find more on this in Chapter 6 on Safety Skills.

Snapchat wants to share each user's location with their in-app friends through Snap Map. To prevent the related geotracking, teach youth to engage Ghost Mode, which makes it looks like the user is offline and excludes them from Snap Map.

10.2 Instagram

Instagram is a visual social network where users can share posts and stories. Posts are available in perpetuity while stories are disappearing content that only remains visible for 24 hours. Those stories can be preserved longer if they are added to the highlights on the profile. Users can also post longer, durable video content to Instagram TV and they can livestream from the platform.

It is recommended youth enable the private account setting so that their content is not visible to all users. Only approved followers will see their Instagram posts and stories.

Instagram content is visual in nature. Users' pictures can be uploaded raw or enhanced with graphics, animations, filters, and adjustments to contrast, color, and brightness.

Within Instagram, other users can be tagged in any shared image. For youth, the tags' placement conveys meaning. Tags on body of person in the photo means they are best friends. People tagged to the left of the person in the image are friends, not best friends. While tags to the right are followers who might be friends or just acquaintances or even strangers.

Further, if you're tagged in a post, youth etiquette requires you to like and comment or there might be social repercussions. In a sense, it's a digital popularity contest. Youth need to be alert to the social pressures of this and empowered to resist the pressure.

Instagram content often includes hashtags that make the content findable for users interested in an endless range of topics. In some cases, hashtags are hijacked for a secondary meaning by a troll, political operative, or promotional campaign. Hijacked hashtags are of concern on Instagram and on other social networks.

And, finally, Instagram posts are often geotagged. If you do not want your youth's location revealed, then require them to turn off location services for this app.

10.3 YouTube

YouTube is a video sharing social network and the second largest search engine behind Google. (Note that YouTube is owned by Google.) Users can watch video content; every minute 4.5 million videos are viewed simultaneously on YouTube. Viewers can vote for content with a thumbs up or thumbs down. In addition, viewers can leave comments and respond to others' comments.

YouTube now offers premium paid content including popular movies and television shows. Youth should be alert to potential spending within the app, especially if they're accessing the site through a parent's account that is connected to a credit card for payment.

Youth may also establish a YouTube channel; a place where they can upload videos in public, unlisted, or private mode. Public videos are available to anyone. Unlisted videos are available to anyone with the link, and private videos can only be seen by those with explicit permission.

Age-inappropriate content is widely available on YouTube. Pornography, violence, and horror content can all be found in ample supply. Parents and teachers can counsel youth to switch on age restrictions and a profanity filter within YouTube. However, youth can just as easily turn those filters off. Ideally, they won't and will avoid much of the inappropriate content with YouTube's content warning.

10.4 TikTok

Officially for users age 13+, TikTok is a video sharing network where users share short videos and can share videos of themselves lip syncing to popular songs. This social network is proving popular with youth, in part, because there is a perception that anyone on the platform has the potential to be internet famous.

This platform includes a digital well being setting where users (or their parents) can program a daily limit on how much the app is used.

Of concern is that TikTok does not currently have a private mode so anyone can follow a youth's account, including strangers. And there are limited, if any, content filters so youth users may hear inappropriate song lyrics or see inappropriate content.

In addition, there have been reports of dangerous challenges on TikTok where users are asked to do unsafe things like the #BrightEye challenge of holding a bag of bleach to your eye or the #BirdBox challenge of navigating the world while blindfolded, as inspired by the movie of the same name. Of course, these challenges pop up in other social networks as well, not just TikTok.

Also note that this app was formerly Music.ly before its new corporate owners rebranded it in 2017. If your youth had a Music.ly account, all their videos are now available on TikTok.

10.5 Facebook

Facebook is the largest social media service. In addition to each user's profile, Facebook users can access pages, groups, and more. Content can be shared in the newsfeed and through Stories, the content that's visible for 24 hours similar to Instagram Stories and SnapChat. The number of youth using Facebook is decreasing as this age group moves to other social media platforms.

Those youth that choose to open Facebook accounts are connecting with friends (and their parents' friends!) on the social platform. The issues of privacy and geotagging arise again but the single sign-on for third-party sites makers it an attractive account for youth. For example, *Wizards Unite*, the latest geo-location game from Niantic, makers of *Pokémon Go* use Facebook and Google to create accounts. There is no option to sign up with an email address directly in the game.

For more ideas, check out Common Sense Media (www.commonsensemedia.org) a nonprofit organization that provides resources to nurture digital citizens in training.

Of course, these social media tools represent but a tiny number of the all the social networks available around the world. And many of those social networks are in non-English languages. WeChat (China), Orkut (Brazil), and VK (Russia and India) to name just three. Check out The Conversation Prism, an infographic that illustrates the scope and scale of social media options available today (https://conversation-prism.com), and know that more options are being added (and others removed) every year.

And, as a reminder, don't forget what you read earlier in Chapter 2 about mental wellness online. Often, social media is the source of digital stress. It's important to reinforce with youth that they have a plan to call for help and that it's OK to go offline and take a break from screen time.

Study Skills

From Grades 6 through 12 in the US and Canada, youth spend thousands of hours completing school projects, essays, and research. Depending on their extracurricular interests, they might also join the debate club, advocate for a social cause, or explore ideas through music, dance, or theater. Hopefully, these educational experiences include lots of experiential learning and an introduction to a wide range of ideas. Inevitably, youth will also be introduced to a variety of digital skills to facilitate and support their learning.

While the exact curriculum varies regionally, students are universally introduced to concepts such as time management, grammar, and note taking. Of course, technology in education varies somewhat to accommodate students' abilities and struggles. For example, some students need a tablet to communicate while others struggle to disconnect from a screen. There's also variation based on each teacher's use of technology in the classroom. Some will embrace it completely, others will resist wholeheartedly, and most will integrate digital elements in their lessons whenever it makes sense given the needs of their students and the available resources.

Overall, study skills ultimately become business skills as youth finish school and move on to jobs and careers. Many youth will transition from high school to further training before embarking on their future careers. No matter their paths — trade school, college, university, industry training — their continued education and, ultimately, their career in the twenty-first century will require digital skills. The journey to that career begins now.

1. Learning Experiences

In school, youth are exposed to a wide range of learning experiences. The traditional classroom lecture is coupled with hands-on experiments, role play, conversation, and debate, and other learning experiences. Overall, today's youth are in school to future-proof their ability to consume, consider, and apply information. What they learn is as important as how they learn so that they can seek out, understand, and apply new information in the future.

With access to more information than ever before, youth must learn to do internet searches and refine them to find the desired information. They must also learn to discern reliable sources from fake news and to understand the nuance of bias within reliable information. With a calculator in their mobile phone, they don't need to master mental math (although they could) but they do need skills to understand the economic implications of taking out a mortgage. Similarly, they can look up the names of those elected to congress or parliament but they need critical thinking skills to understand political decisions. Those same critical thinking skills will serve them well when they research historical events and consider them in the current context. For example, in Canada, the culture and history of aboriginal peoples is being restored through the recommendations of the Truth and Reconciliation Commission, yet students still find decades of information that suppressed aboriginals' heritage.

As Charlotte Glease noted, "We will need people who are prepared to ask, and answer, the questions that aren't Googleable: like what are the ethical ramifications of machine automation? What are the political consequences of mass unemployment? How should we distribute wealth in a digitised society? As a society we need to be more philosophically engaged." (*The Guardian*, January 9, 2017). She goes on to suggest that students should be learning philosophy to learn to ask and answer these thoughtful, unsearchable questions.

2. Reading and Writing

Before youth get to philosophy lessons or critical thinking problems, they do need to master the basics of reading and writing. By Grade

6, most youth have learned the basics of both. During middle school and high school, youth expand their skills in both areas. They learn more vocabulary, explore more complex literary devices, and refine their grasp of grammar, spelling, and punctuation. Ultimately, youth should be able to do research to inform themselves and have the skills to consume and communicate in words.

At a younger age, youth may have experienced *Reading Rainbow*, a digital literacy television show that evolved into an online community with reading resources that embrace technology. Spokesperson (and *Star Trek* actor) Levar Burton had this to say: "We're all about using technology. Television was simply the technology we used back in the day. If you want to reach kids today, you need to be on the digital devices that they want to be on. We are all about utilizing technology to engage kids, and we know from experience, from five years of data, that it works. Kids come to the Skybrary to read and to watch our educational video field trips. They feel it's a world they want to be in, and that's what we want." (*EdTech Magazine*, January 12, 2017). Meanwhile, other families may have emphasized offline reading with regular visits to the bookstore or library to ensure a steady supply of fiction and non-fiction reading material.

Reading will be in competition with social media, videos, and games to garner youth's attention. And what they read will be a combination of short-form and long-form work from quick social media posts and text messages to full-length novels and blog series. Overall, youth need to be encouraged to consume a wide range of information on a wide range of topics; a well-rounded education, if you will.

Putting their own thoughts into words requires a different sort of practice. To be a good writer requires practice and constructive feedback. At school, much of that formative feedback comes from teachers as they mark student submissions. However, the submissions can be better if they learn to use technology to help refine the mechanics of their writing.

Built into most word-processing programs, **spell check** flags misspelled words and offers suggestions to correct the spelling. Of course, students' first attempt to spell the word must be close enough to the real word to get the correct spelling. For example, if a student misspells "fabulous" as "fibulas," spell check won't find the error as fibulas is the plural of fibula, a bone in the lower leg.

Similarly, students writing in English will discover their word processor offers spellcheck for American English and British English. Some will also offer Canadian English, typically a blend of American and British spellings. So students might note the color gray in the United States but the correct spelling in many British and Canadian English dictionaries is grey, with an e. Hundreds of other words have American/British variations including color/colour, center/centre, licence/license, dialog/dialogue, and so on. The key is for youth to become aware of the issue and learn to set the language preference in their word processor to the version their teachers expect them to use.

A close cousin to spell check is **grammar check**, a tool that helps students construct grammatically correct phrases, clauses, sentences, and paragraphs. The software looks at each word in context with the surrounding words and tries to understand the writer's intention. While not foolproof, this tool can help students achieve subject/verb agreement, clarify word order, avoid split infinitives, and other helpful fixes. Of course, grammar check is not a perfect tool as the errors detected may not be errors if the software has misunderstood the writer's meaning. As youth use grammar check, they also learn grammar so that they gain confidence as to when to challenge the recommendations.

As a student's vocabulary expands, they will encounter unfamiliar words. Given the media-rich environments they live in online, it's highly probable that they will hear a word and not know how to spell it. If they can sound it out and guess, a **dictionary** can help. While many schools still require students to have a paperback copy of *Merriam Webster's* or some other dictionary, writers are more likely to turn to an internet search, a dictionary app, or a website for help. Youth need to learn how to search for words and their variations (plurals, different verb tenses, etc.) through these tools. In addition, a digital **thesaurus** can help youth figure out synonyms to put more variety in their writing.

Beyond spelling conventions, there are dozens of **style guides** that dictate the "correct" form of writing. While youth are mostly focused on the basics of spelling, grammar, and paragraph construction, their teachers may introduce a simple style guide. Each guide notes writing conventions that will be applied. Examples include use of the Oxford comma, what words to capitalize, how to format acronyms, and so on. As youth move into senior high school, their teachers may introduce the formal style guides they'll use in college or university. There are dozens to choose from but three of the most common are the American Psychological Association (APA), Modern Language Association

(MLA), and *The Chicago Manual of Style*, all of which come in print and electronic formats.

Writing for the web has style, too. As youth learn to communicate digitally, they learn @mentions, #hashtags, alt-text, CamelCase, and similar. They might also learn about cascading style sheets (CSS), HTML, embed code, hyperlinks, and more. Youth also have a language for text messages and using emojis.

Finally, youth need to learn how to write **citations** to give credit for other people's intellectual property they might quote in their writing. By learning to include references, youth learn to share ideas in their own words supplemented by quotes from other people's work. Digital information makes it easy to cut and paste answers. As a result, it can be tempting to use someone else's words. Learning to resist this temptation and give credit where credit is due is a vital digital life skill. Youth learn to credit the source in informal ways at first, by sharing a link to the source or noting the author's name, where their words were first published, and the date. Over time, youth will learn more formal citations as mapped out in the style guide they are asked to use.

By using these tools, students can refine their writing to minimize mechanical errors creating more opportunities for teachers to provide constructive feedback on the information they've gathered, the arguments they've constructed, and the bias they've presented.

3. School Communication

For middle school and high school age students, passing notes is almost a rite of passage. While today's tweens and teens are using technology to communicate, their parents and teachers will remember doing the same with bits of paper. From cloud-based apps such as Google Docs and OneNote to chat apps such as WhatsApp and Facebook Messenger to social media apps such as TikTok and Snapchat, there's always a way to pass along a note. Students find ways to communicate with friends before, during, and after class.

Take, for example, Google Docs. As Taylor Lorenz reported, teens told her they use "Google Docs to chat just about any time they need to put their phone away but know their friends will be on computers.

Sometimes they'll use the service's live-chat function, which doesn't open by default, and which many teachers don't even know exists." (*The Atlantic*, March 14, 2019). While this discovery is in itself a digital skill, the broader digital life skill is teaching youth how/when it is appropriate to communicate with one another.

While youth have social motivations to communicate with friends, they also have many practical reasons to communicate with teachers, school administrators, and fellow students. Whether they need to send a teacher homework by email, look up the office phone number to tell the school office they have a doctor's appointment, or reach out to classmates assigned to the same group project, communication is key. To do so, youth need to know how to use more formal communication tools.

Many schools issue every student an **email** address, some as early as Grade 4. Those schools that don't assume students will set up a free email account on a service such as Gmail. Once set up, students must learn how to use the to/cc/bcc fields to address each email and how to fill in the subject line. They also need to learn to include attachments and the potential limitations for large file sizes. And they've got to learn to write the text of the email itself in a business-like manner with a formal greeting, body text, and closing. They may also want to set up a signature so that every message ends with their name and basic contact information or other details (e.g., student number).

Crafting an email is only one layer of the digital skills to be mastered. Youth must also learn to manage their emails. This includes checking for messages regularly and replying, as necessary. Youth will also want to declutter their data by ensuring they deal with each message. Some messages will be deleted while others will be archived for future reference.

They'll also need to learn how to manage spam and how to be alert for suspicious messages. They won't know to avoid links or attachments from strangers or with unusual file formats if they aren't introduced to these risks.

I've been an advocate for digital decluttering for several years now. If youth are struggling to manage their email or other elements of their digital footprint, you'll find more resources to help them in my earlier book, *Declutter Your Data* (Self-Counsel Press, 2018).

While, anecdotally, youth today prefer to communicate by text message, they also have to master the art of the **phone**. The mechanics of placing or answering a call on their mobile phone is a good first step. And if their phone plan includes things like three-way calling, call waiting, or voicemail, you'll need to make sure they know how to use these features as well.

Once they've mastered the mechanics, youth may also need guidance about the call itself. They need to learn that there's no need to shout into the phone! And if they are on public transit, it might not be a good time for a long phone call out of consideration for other passengers. They also need to know the impacts of background noise. Other people talking nearby, wind across the headset microphone, and other audio can make it hard for the recipient to hear the caller.

All of these phone skills flow over to digital chats, as well. Voice to voice conversations on Discord or other audio-enabled chat apps and video chats on Zoom, Skype, FaceTime, and the like share similar etiquette. While school administrators may not be available on Skype, peers working on the same group project will be. And workplace standards are shifting to digital solutions.

Messages can come from so many different places and platforms today. Text messages, emails, direct messages inside Twitter, LinkedIn, Snapchat, Instagram, WhatsApp, Facebook Messenger, and many more. Part of learning to communicate in the digital age is about learning to keep up with the notifications and find ways to stay in touch without being overwhelmed by it all. Parents and teachers can guide youth in developing healthy digital communication habits. This likely means using dedicated times to respond to messages (and then a habit of getting away from the screen and doing something else for awhile). Youth can also be empowered to make it clear that they do not correspond on certain platforms. They can say no to TikTok or any other platform.

And, as we look to the future, communication tools will offer interoperability; a blending of platforms so that users can be on different platforms but still connect seamlessly. At Social Media Camp 2019, Mari Smith talked about the likely integration of Facebook Messenger, WhatsApp, and Instagram direct messages in her keynote presentation. The benefit is that users will be able to communicate more easily across platforms. Of course, youth need to talk to their teachers, school administrators, and peers using the tools available today. But learning these digital skills will prepare them for future shifts in digital communications.

4. Note Taking

Technology provides several ways for students to take notes. The simplest is to use pencil and paper to take handwritten notes. (Yes, both pencil and paper are technologies!) Other options include typing notes, audio recording, video recording, and, even using a stylus to take digital handwritten notes.

Handwritten notes tend to be best for retention. The action of writing the words on the page helps us commit those ideas to memory. Meanwhile, typed notes are more legible and more easily shared with others. And, if the student has learned to touch type, this method can be faster than handwriting.

Does your school teach the art of touch typing? A formal introduction to ready position over the asdf jkl; keys and related muscle memory of the entire alphabet can help youth move beyond hunt-and-peck typing on a keyboard to a more efficient typing style. Of course, youth also develop stellar two-thumb typing on their mobile phones. While typing may seem like a dying art in the age of voice dictation, it's not always practical to take voice notes. Imagine the chaos during class if all 30 students dictated their notes while the teacher was giving the lesson! Learning to touch type is a recommended digital skill if only for the silence in class and, more importantly, the health benefits of minimizing the potential for repetitive strain injuries.

All methods of data input come with risk of a repetitive stress injury. Formal touch typing can contribute to carpal tunnel in the wrists and forearms. Thumb typing can trigger repetitive stress injuries in the thumbs and hands. Meanwhile, voice dictation can strain the vocal cords. Introduce youth to the early warning signs of these types of injuries so that they can seek help before them become chronic conditions. Periods of rest and simple stretches can alleviate symptoms. No one should have to live permanently with the burning sensation of carpal tunnel or other injuries.

When it comes to note taking, youth may focus on a simple organizational system of notebooks or Duo-Tangs, one for each subject. If they type their notes, digital file folders can be organized by subject or project. More complex, media rich notes can be taken using a note taking app. These apps offer the opportunity to capture text, links, images, audio, and video and the information can be synchronized between devices. This is helpful if students are using a school computer, home computer, and mobile phone to keep track of their work.

Evernote and Google Keep are both note-taking apps. They offer different but similar functionality, including voice dictation. They have the added benefits of tagging or labeling which allows youth to group information in ways that it can be searched easily. And, these tools allow you to link reminders to your calendar apps so that project meetings and homework deadlines can be part of the student's calendar.

5. Web Research

In their studies and at home, youth will frequently turn to search engines to look for information. While entering keywords into the search box will bring them results, adult mentors can introduce them to the following super-search skills for their next visit to Google.

- Instinctively, users search for **keywords** and keyword phrases that describe what they are looking for. The more specific the words, the better the results. For example, try looking up "soup" or "chicken noodle soup."

- **Stop words** are short words that search engines have been programmed to ignore. Examples include the, a, an, the, and in. If a user includes these words in their search terms, the search engine will skip over these words when it looks for matching results. For example, "the chicken soup recipe" will garner the same results as "chicken soup recipe."

- **Boolean search** allows users to modify the search with one of three operators (modifying words) — AND, NOT, OR. By putting one of these words between a search keyword or keyword phrase users indicate to the search engine the results you want to see. For example, "chicken soup AND recipe." Another option, might be "chicken OR turkey soup recipe."

- **Quotation marks** can also be helpful to tell the search engine which words are a keyword phrase. For example, "chicken soup recipe." Quotes are especially helpful when using Boolean search. For example, "chicken OR turkey" AND "soup recipe."

- **Dashes** can be used to note keywords you want excluded from a search. This is similar to the Boolean search term NOT. For example, use soup recipe -chicken to find a soup recipe for anything but chicken soup.

- **Tilde** is used to instruct the search engine to use synonyms. For example, a search for ~poultry soup would bring up recipes for soup made with chicken, turkey, duck, and goose.

- **Two periods** between two numbers are used to search for a range of numbers. This is helpful if you're looking for information from a particular date range, price range, or measurement. For example, chicken soup 1939..1945 would show results for chicken soup recipes during World War II.

- **Site:query** is used to limit the search to a specific website. For example, chicken soup site:bonappetit.com shows only recipes from *Bon Appetit*, a food magazine.

- **Link:query** is used to limit the search to a specific website and websites linked to it. For example, chicken soup link:nytimes.com shows recipes on *The New York Times* website and any other website that links to *The New York Times*.

- **Related:query** is used to find sites related to a particularly website. For example, a search for related:cnn.com shows results that include other major news outlets including *Time Magazine*, *USA Today*, *Washington Post*, and more.

Once youth learn how to do a search, they need guidance to know how to interpret the search engine results page (SERP). First, they need to know that the results near the top of the page will often be paid search results. In Google search, these are currently noted with a tiny square icon that reads "ad." Next, they need to know that search results are grouped by type. By default, all search results are shown but the user can narrow the search results to show just images, video, maps, and so on.

This section focuses on the Google search engine because it is the most widely used search engine. As of January 2019, 73 percent of all searches were done using Google. Bing (8 percent) and Yahoo (4 percent) are the next most popular search engines and then there are dozens more. Some offer unique features like DuckDuckGo's emphasis on privacy. (www.reliablesoft. net/top-10-search-engines-in-the-world, accessed July, 2019).

Once they learn to find the organic search results, youth learn to judge the quality of the websites they visit. This takes practice as they learn to identity and assess several factors including:

- Who wrote the information?
- What is goal of the website?
- Does the information support the goals?
- Can I check these facts?
- Is this balanced information offering two or more perspectives?
- Is the author clearly identified or is the information from an anonymous source?
- What's their bias?
- Is the date of publication recent or old?
- Is it relevant to your situation?

When a big news story breaks, check online for the latest information and then check back in a few minutes, then a longer gap, and so on. New information will take time to be reported by reputable sites. There's no need to click refresh on your browser continuously. Similarly, to keep up to date, you can't not check in at all. Teach youth to follow news outlets on Twitter or to scan the headlines of leading news organizations' websites. My son, at age 11, started reading news headlines daily to learn more about regional, national, and international news. Today, he uses Apple News to curate media coverage on topics of interest and headlines from his preferred news outlets.

It's also important for youth to know how to do some research without the internet. Eileen Velthuis, book editor and mother of two, showed her kids how to use an encyclopedia to find information. Similarly, a dictionary and thesaurus are useful offline tools to learn just in case the power is out, the internet is down, or something else is keeping youth offline. Limited screen time, perhaps?

6. Identifying Fake News and Bias

As parents and teachers mentor emerging digital citizens, youth must be introduced to the concepts of fake news and bias. In simple terms, fake news is the incorrect reporting of facts. Bias is the perspective of the report and how it impacts the interpretation of the facts. As youth explore online information, you can equip them with tools to help them evaluate a source in the context of fake news and bias. These websites will help:

- **Snopes** (www.snopes.com) is the world's leading fact checking site and frequent stop for anyone doing online research. Its mission is to fight misinformation across the internet by prioritizing evidence-based reporting provided in context. It also helps identify frequently shared, viral content that is based on urban legends, hoaxes, and folklore.

- **Politifact** (www.politifact.com) assesses statements of politicians, candidates, bureaucrats, and other newsmakers using their trademarked Truth-o-Meter™. Focused mainly on US politics, each story is assessed for its veracity on a scale of false : mostly false : half true : mostly true : true. They also note "full flop" when someone reverses their position on an issue.

- **Factcheck.org** (www.factcheck.org) also monitors United States politics with a critical look at speeches, press releases, and other content through a lens of journalistic and scholarly integrity.

- **Media Bias Fact Check** (mediabiasfactcheck.com) is "dedicated to educating the public on media bias and deceptive news practices." Visitors can search for any topic and the search results note MBFC's bias rating. Bias is noted on a scale of left bias : left-center bias : least biased : right-center bias : right bias : pro science : conspiracy pseudoscience : questionable sources : satire : re-evaluated sources.

It can also be helpful to introduce youth to vague and ambiguous language that indicates the news being published online isn't definite. Examples of vague language include words like probably, about, sort of, and more. For example, using vague language, "about 20 students went on the field trip." In contrast, specific language would state, "The art gallery field trip was attended by 22 students."

Furthermore, we have to teach youth to be discerning about what they see online. Is that viral video telling the whole story? Or has the information been taken out of context? For example, in January 2019 a viral video showed a Covington Catholic High School student wearing a red "Make America Great Again" ball cap seemingly mock an Omaha tribal elder near the Lincoln Memorial. While that clip went viral and invoked global outrage for the student's behavior, later information suggested that the students had also been provoked and bullied in the time leading up to the viral clip.

The bigger message is articulated well by Ian Bogost, "Despite the widespread creation and dissemination of video online, people still seem to believe that cameras depict the world as it really is; the truth comes from finding the right material from the right camera. That idea is mistaken, and it's bringing forth just as much animosity as the polarization that is thought to produce the conflicts cameras record." (*The Atlantic*, January 21, 2019.) As parents and teachers raising digital youth, part of your job is to explain how media can be manipulated to tell a story from a certain point of view.

As youth learn to interpret online media, you can encourage their efforts by introducing the notion of bias. Take time to explain common types of bias and look for teachable moments to discuss examples with youth when they occur.

- **Confirmation bias** occurs when you favor information that supports your existing knowledge. This type of bias is problematic because you stop looking for new information if the initial information reinforces your existing point of view.

- **Filter bubble** occurs when a social media algorithm or search engine shows you information related to your past online actions. Your search history, friend connections, and even the type of computer or mobile phone you use influence the information you see creating a filter on the information readily available to you.

- **Belief bias** occurs when you accept information that is plausible. In other words, if information is believable you accept it as true. This idea creates challenges because you can't set aside your current belief to consider something that's new.

- **In-group bias** occurs when you favor information from people or sources that are part of your usual circles, your in-group. The opposite of in-group is out-group. This favoritism gives more weight to information coming from your in-group and discounts information from any out-group.

- **Optimism bias** occurs when you have an overly positive view of the information. More than just a positive attitude, this type of bias results in unrealistic positive thinking. It's opposite, **pessimism bias** occurs when you have an overly negative view that results in unrealistic negative thinking.

- **Selection bias** occurs when information is gathered from a sample of people that are not representative of the population.

- **Omission bias** occurs when sources that represent a point of view are deliberately excluded from a news report. For example, a balanced article about new school construction should include facts and opinions from school administrators, teachers, parents, and students.

- **The halo effect** occurs when sources that are considered good are assumed to always be good. This effect can be triggered by a news outlets overall reporting reputation or, simply, by the attractive physical appearance of a reporter.

- **The framing effect** occurs when you are unduly influenced by the way information is shared. The context can be manipulated to lead you to a certain point of view.

Overall, parents and teachers can help youth develop best practices when it comes to information found online. Encourage them to verify a story before you share it in their school work or through social media. While we're all guilty of sharing something without thinking, we can highlight why this can be problematic and explain that it's not okay to assume every item is correct and share it anyway. It's important for youth to know that the number of times an article has been shared doesn't make it true. If your friends are saying the same thing, it doesn't make it true (this is confirmation bias). The best way to be sure is to do your own research from several trusted resources covering the same story. It's also helpful to keep this framework in mind, what category does the piece fall into?

- News or fake news
- Sponsored information
- Opinion piece
- Advertorial
- Propaganda
- Satire
- Entertainment

Fake news may also include fake opinions in the form of fake reviews. Recall the information in Chapter 3 where you read about fake reviews in the context of online finances and online shopping.

7. Productivity and Organization

To complete any school year, youth need systems to be productive and keep their information organized. As the volume of homework increases and size of assignments grows, students have more and more to manage.

As with many things in this book, there are analog solutions. A notebook and pencil can be used to create to-do lists and tasks can be tracked in a planner or on a wall calendar. And there's a special satisfaction in crossing a completed item off the list or tagging it with an emphatic checkmark. However, some youth will prefer a digital solution so that they don't have to remember their paper list.

Many apps are available to help people stay organized. To begin, youth need a calendar to manage appointments and deadlines. There are lots of options to choose from: Google Calendar, iCal, Outlook, or some other calendar software. Which software to use might be influenced by what other family members use or what the school uses. If teachers are using Google's G Suite for Education or Microsoft's Office 365, students may need to use that tool to access the shared calendar and other information. Youth might need to keep track of:

- Class schedules

- Tumbling timetables

- Homework assignments

- Project milestones

- School activities

- Exams

- Holidays

- Non-instructional days

No matter which calendar program they use, youth will be able to make appointments for events that are time and date specific. They'll also learn to create repeating events for activities that happen every day/week/month. And they'll learn to create events that cross a span of days without a time specific activity — say the exam period for each semester.

Beyond their personal calendar, encourage youth to find out if their school has an app. The app may include school events that can be synchronized.

As youth learn to manage their own calendars, they learn not only how to record deadlines, but how to do the work in advance of the deadline so that they are prepared to turn in assignments, or bring information to a promised meeting.

And speaking of that information, youth have to learn how to organize their files. As they learn how, they'll figure out file-naming conventions, folder structure, version control, etc. They may also need to learn to do electronic paperwork for school and extracurricular activities.

Be sure to introduce youth to the necessities of data back-ups and document synchronization. Storing school work or other files on their laptop's hard drive is risky as files can be damaged or lost if the computer is broken or stolen. Help them set up cloud storage on Dropbox, Google Drive, or One Drive to create a central place to keep their files. This is a convenient way for them to access their study files at school and at home. But, also alert them to the potential for sync errors as there is a brief time lag between upload and download between devices and sometimes the sync fails.

8. Creativity

While the advice in this chapter has focused on practical, tangible study skills, creativity also has a place in a digital life. Encourage youth that do well with technology and have an interest in creative pursuits to use some of their screen time to write, record, and create. "While today's apps provide unparalleled tools for connecting, communicating, and advocating, perhaps we should follow artist Björk's advice to "put humanity into technology," to use it to "be more creative," and "a little less for memes." ("björk says we all need to get off facebook and go for a walk," i-d.vice.com, May 9, 2017). Happily, Howard Gardner and Katie Davis' research supports this notion. "[They found] that digital media open up new avenues for youth to express themselves creatively. Remix, collage, video production, and music composition — to name just a few popular artistic genres of the day — are easier and cheaper for today's youth to pursue than were their predigital counterparts. It's also easier to find an audience for one's creative productions." (*The App Generation: How Today's Youth Navigate Identity, Intimacy, and Imagination in a Digital World*, Yale University Press, 2013.)

Aspiring writers can hone their skills with a blog, poetry, prose, or any unconstrained written format they want to explore. Many online writers' groups offer daily or monthly writing prompts. Tools like Tumblr give youth an opportunity to create virtual worlds where they can experiment with complex settings, character development, plot driven stories, and more.

Similarly, audio and video recording gives youth opportunities to explore their voice and their ability to tell stories. Whether they are documenting a local ecological crisis or in conversation with peers about LGBTQ+ activism or want to create a fan version of the latest Marvel movie, they can begin with the tools in their mobile phone to record and edit both audio and video. Even better, if desired, they can upload their creations as a podcast or to YouTube to share with an audience.

These same tools can be used by aspiring musicians. They may choose to write and record original music, remix existing music, or participate in online communities' creative efforts. (Check out Eric Whitacre's virtual youth choir for an example.) TikTok and other platforms create a karaoke-like experiences for singers to practice and showcase their favorite tunes.

And let's not forget the visual arts. From a relaxing color-by-number art experiences to freehand drawing tools like the Apple Pencil on an iPad, youth can use technology to create, enhance, and even animate their 2-D creations. And those same creative skills can be extended to test the capacity of a 3-D printer to create sculptures, figurines, fan art, and more.

Of course, creative potential isn't limited to the performing and visual arts. Get creative in the garden, on the water, or in the kitchen. Rebecca Coleman, for example, includes her teenage son in some of the culinary adventures that feed her Cooking by Laptop blog (http://cookingbylaptop.com) and its supporting social media channels. Ms. Coleman notes, "We see a lot of doom and gloom online about how too much screen time is turning our kids' brains into goo. While I'm not for raising hermits who only interact with the world through a computer screen, we also need to be aware of and celebrate the creativity and connections our kids can find online. My son has an active YouTube channel, and has found a real passion for creating and connecting with other creative kids online through platforms like Steam and Deviant Art." (interview, June 2019). Author Anya Kamentz agrees, "the amazing things that happen when kids take advantage of the infinite worlds available to them to do deep dives on their interests and teach themselves new skills. These can include designing apps and websites, of course, but also writing and sharing stories, drawing pictures, shooting and editing videos, animation, making and remixing music, or modifying video games." (*The Art of Screen Time: How Your Family Can Balance Digital Media & Real Life*, PublicAffairs Hachette Book Group, 2018).

With all this creative potential, youth also need time to explore and consume other's creativity from professional artists and their friends. They can cheer on their peers, share feedback and make suggestions, or simply enjoy the work as patrons of the arts in training.

Safety Skills

No book about digital life skills would be complete without saying something about safety. The internet is full of potential perils and you must teach youth ways to protect themselves online.

While cyberbullying, catfishing, luring, and other nefarious behaviors do happen online, most youth deal with different safety issues; distracted driving, for example.

Parents and teachers are often scared when they read headlines such as "72 percent of victims of cyberbullying are age 13 or older" or "45 percent of teens asked to send nude photos were under age 15." The problem is these sensational headlines evoke emotions before the reader can think critically about the facts. How many victims are there? Adults are over age 13, too, are they included in this statistic? While there's no question these things do happen to some degree, most youth will never encounter them except in a lesson about cyber safety.

By equipping youth with digital safety skills, your goal is to make best efforts to prevent an incident, especially a critical incident. You won't be able to protect them from all the dangers of the world. This is true offline just as much as it's true online. But we can teach them to do the internet equivalent of looking both ways before they cross the street. As Sean Smith, social media educator and Air Cadet Training Officer, remarked, "It's shortsighted to default to the fear factor when it comes to youth and technology. You aren't equipping youth for the future if you wrap them in bubble wrap. " While the focus of this chapter is on awareness and prevention, you'll find resources noted in the book to help if someone in your family or a student in your class needs help.

1. Digital Responsibility

First and foremost, we have to show our kids what digital responsibility is. Modeling the best behavior isn't always easy. Pause for a moment and contemplate if you've ever used your mobile phone while driving without a hands-free device. Or used an open Wi-Fi network and logged into your bank account anyway. Or maybe you've sent your spouse a nude photo or received one in return. Adults make poor choices sometimes and take responsibility for the consequences, whether that means a hefty traffic fine for distracted driving or the embarrassment of a coworker seeing your naked body. Youth haven't yet learned how to navigate that responsibility.

The best way forward is to model digital responsibility for youth. Put the phone away when driving. Keep nudity offline. And so on. Sometimes it's about not circulating harmful information. There's a great example from the television series *Mythbusters* when cohost Adam Savage revealed at a fan Q&A that the *Mythbusters* team had tested an everyday substance that is so explosive they destroyed the footage and agreed never to talk about what they learned. ("Mythbusters Destroyed All Evidence of an Easy to Make Explosive," Nerdist. com, March 29, 2016.)

Here is a trusted adult with influence over millions of fans making it clear that some information shouldn't be shared. Parents and teachers can do the same on a smaller scale.

So, what is digital responsibility? Youth learn that it is not an inherent right to have technology. Rather, digital responsibility is the acceptable and appropriate use of technology. It's about learning to use devices in a safe manner (no distracted driving or bike riding!) and how to use software and apps without harming themselves or anyone else. And it's about knowing how and when to use technology in a true emergency. Even simple things like calling 911 need context so that youth don't abuse the emergency line but still feel empowered to dial 911 when emergency services are needed.

2. Community Alerts

When it comes to safety, knowing what's happening locally is an essential defense. Middle schools, high schools, and colleges leverage social media and, sometimes, a customized safety app to send alerts about issues on campus. Whether they use Twitter, Facebook, or an app, youth can be alerted to power outages, construction closures, icy conditions, transit interruptions, and more. Alarmingly, they can also be used to distribute information about intruders and active shooters on school property. On college campuses, these same tools can be used to facilitate safewalk programs and other on-campus personal safety supports.

To ensure youth have access to this information, help them find and download their school's app or support them in setting up a Twitter account to follow the school or school district's tweets. It is also helpful to show them how to bookmark the school website so that they can find that information quickly when needed.

Similarly, it's also a good idea to alert youth to the existence of an emergency alert system. In theory, in the event of a major emergency — wildfire, earthquake, tornado — government agencies in many areas will send information and instructions to all smartphones via text message. Usually, each message also comes with a loud alert tone or beep to draw community members' attention to the incoming information. Inform youth that they will likely receive a test message from time to time. There is an image of a recent one from the Province of British Columbia in Figure 1.

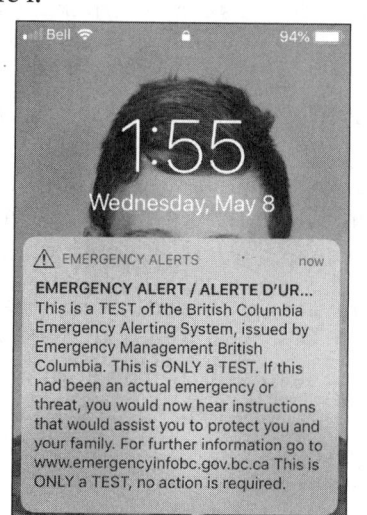

Figure 1: Emergency Alert Text Graphic

When your community does a test of the emergency alert system, check in with youth at home or in class. Did they get the test message? Would they know what to do, if it had been a real emergency?

"The immediacy of smartphone communication — and the extent to which we're glued to our mobile devices — have made them an important resource for governments developing warning systems about potential natural disasters." (CBC News, January 29, 2018.) If youth are allowed a device of their own, let's empower them to be effective in an emergency.

But if you live in an area that is at risk for a tsunami or earthquake, [Peter Anderson, an associate professor with Simon Fraser University's school of communication said], being reachable should be a priority. "Maybe that means at least one person in the household always has their phone on," he said.

3. Identity Theft

Identity theft occurs when someone knowingly uses another person's identity. Usually, this is done for financial gain by fraudulently accessing the victim's bank accounts and credit cards. As youth grow up, you can teach them some basic habits that help protect against identity theft.

First, teach youth to safeguard their snail mail and keep track of their paper trail — both incoming and outgoing. Incoming papers might include notices from school, bank statements, and pay stubs. Any document that includes personal information should be guarded carefully. This includes anything that shows a name, address, and/or phone number, including envelopes. Some documents may also include youth's social security number (USA), social insurance number (Canada), personal education number, student identification number, or other identifiers. Make it a family responsibility to be alert to household bills and travel documents in the same way. Even a phone bill or a boarding pass has personal information on it.

Outgoing papers must be shredded when those documents are no longer needed to secure personal information. Simply putting them in the trash or recycling leaves the person at risk of identity theft. As much as possible, request documents be sent as e-post or downloadables to reduce the risk of theft from your mailbox. Keep track of the physical papers that arrive in your home or at school.

Next, encourage youth to protect their smartphones. Password protection makes it harder for thieves to access information. For some apps, you can turn on two-factor authentication to make it even harder for scammers to access your data.

If youth have computers, these need protection, too. Encourage them to keep their operating system (OS) up-to-date to ensure they have the latest security support. An older OS might have a vulnerability that can be exploited. In addition, use a firewall, virtual private network, and/or antivirus software for additional protection.

Think carefully about using public Wi-Fi with smartphones and other devices. These networks are typically open and anyone with the right tools and skills can see information shared across them with ease. Teach your teen to avoid online shopping and banking tasks over public Wi-Fi networks. Even typing a password to any account is an action that can be logged.

Of course, shopping in brick and mortar stores also requires some digital savvy. At the checkout, teach your teen to guard their PIN as they pay for items. Make sure their PINs are strong; scammers will try easy guesses like 1234 to use your payment cards. And now that RFID technology makes "tap & pay" convenient, it's extra important that shoppers keep their credit cards and debit cards in sight at all times when making a transaction. For further protection, invest in a wallet, purse, or backpack with RFID blocking to protect payment cards when not in use.

Youth will need guidance on how to detect and avoid a scammer's email. While spam filters will stop many messages, a few will get through. Often, at first glance, they look like legitimate emails from known brands. Teach youth to inspect a suspect email; look for oddly phrased copy, typos, spacing errors, and, most of all, unofficial email addresses and web links.

Social media is another great resource for identity thieves. Encourage kids and teens to keep their profiles private not public. Advise them to be cautious about what they share online. Family vacations announced on Facebook broadcast that your home is empty and unattended. And online quizzes and fun questions can inadvertently reveal dates and years of birth, mother's maiden name, and other personal details that help identity thieves steal.

Girl Scouts have added a CyberSecurity badge, one of dozens of badges focused on science, technology, engineering, and math (STEM) topics. "Launched in late January [2019], the curriculum teaches Junior Girl Scouts about online security issues, including protecting their personal information and dealing with cyberbullying." (*Spark*, CBC Radio, March 17, 2019.)

4. Navigating Nudity

For youth, their identity is, in part, wrapped up in their changing bodies. As they enter puberty and navigate the hormonal, physical, and psychological changes of the teen years, youth experience a wide range of issues from learning to live with periods and ejaculation to learning to accept their bodies. As part of that awakening between childhood and adulthood, youth become aware of nudity and the differences between their bodies and other people's.

When it comes to nudity online, youth are navigating two separate but related issues: sexually explicit content and sexual solicitation. The former includes unwanted exposure to naked or lurid photos, commonly known as pornography, through search engine search results, text messages, and social media. In contrast, youth may experience sexual solicitation through requests for nude or semi-nude photos of themselves. "Approximately one in five youth experience unwanted online exposure to sexually explicit material and one in nine youth experience online sexual solicitation." (*University of Calgary* research team, www.jahonline.org/article/S1054-139X(18)30134-4/abstract, accessed June, 2019).

Northwestern University doctoral candidate Sara Thomas' research affirms that teens are being asked to provide nude photographs by their peers. "Sexting, or sending sexually suggestive images or messages to others, is a reality for an estimated 15 to 25 percent of teens growing up in the digital age. Though some research points to sexting as a potentially low-risk way to explore sexuality, the practice also is associated with increased risk of ostracism, depression, and suicide." (blog, School of Education and Social Policy [SESP], Northwestern University, December 6, 2017,). Ms. Thomas' research goes on to affirm that teenagers struggle to say no when asked for nudes.

With youth, nudity and sexuality are issues in part because youth are too young to give informed consent. They may not even understand what consent is and what it means. I've always liked the "tea and consent" analogy developed by the Thames Valley Police. A short animated video helps, "If you're still struggling with consent just imagine instead of initiating sex you're making them a cup of tea." You'll find the video on YouTube: https://youtu.be/pZwvrxVavnQ or simply search for "consent and tea." It's suitable for all ages and illustrates consent in simple terms.

Coercion is also an issue for youth navigating nudity. Youth need to understand that if someone tries to persuade them to do anything (including sharing nudes) by threatening bodily harm, social ostracizing, or other consequences then this is coercion. Sometimes this behavior is referred to as sextortion or sexploitation. By any name, it's not okay. This is a key area where youth's mental wellness is at risk when they are online.

So, how can parents and teachers help youth navigate the nudity? Explain "A nude is a naked, or partially naked, photo." Then, have a family conversation about nudity. It's a tricky balance that will be influenced by each family's values and beliefs. For all families, the goal is to help youth feel comfortable with their bodies while also making it clear that it is illegal to request or distribute nude photographs. Make sure they understand that even a supposedly private message that includes a nude image is against the law when the person in the picture is a minor (under the age of majority). Set ground rules that make it clear that asking for nude photos and distributing nudes online is not OK. For many teens, the simple parental authority of such rules will empower them to make the right choice.

Of course, teens cannot control what they receive so they also need to know what to do when they receive such requests. A family's approach to this issue will be moderated by their cultural and community values about sexuality, premarital sex, gender politics, and more. In all situations, documenting the request is key. A simple screenshot is the first line of defense to note evidence of inappropriate requests.

Taking a screenshot to document the request is a good first step. Next, teens must know that they can and should report the request. This also applies to any nude image sent to them. It is against the law in Canada and the United States (as well as other places around the world), to distribute nude photographs of minors. So, even those bathtub photos of toddlers frolicking in the bubbles have the potential to be unlawful.

Inform youth in your life that you are willing to hear about requests for nudity and unsolicited nude images received. Youth must know they can tell a trusted parent, guardian, teacher, or other adult. In turn, that trusted adult can help them record the request and report the incident to the authorities. Contact your local police department for guidance or visit a national service like CyperTip Canada at www. cybertip.ca/app/en.

To prevent the need for such reports, youth need to know they can decline requests for nudes; even if they are threatened with consequences for failing to comply. No means no. And youth need to know they'll have support from friends, family, and teachers. A local police department shared a graphic that teens could use to respond to nude requests with an emphatic "no!" As that image has since been removed from their resource page, we've developed the image in Figure 2 (available on the download kit), that youth can use as needed.

Figure 2

Of course, as with all things digital, the role of nudity and sexuality in our lives is a bigger topic. We use social media and other channels to encourage youth to celebrate their bodies and embrace their emerging sexuality. How can we teach youth about nudes and sex in their digital lives in a way that honors them as they grow up to be sexually active adults while still protecting them from predators and reputation issues?

5. Online Safety

More than any other topic, online safety has been written about over and over again. There are seemingly endless articles, books, and speakers all talking about the risks for youth online and our collective need to keep them safe. Often these materials are more sensational than practical. Let's pause and acknowledge that these issues are worrying, even scary. Then, let's refocus on what we can teach youth to help them develop the digital skills they need to stay safe online.

There are a series of common topics when we talk about online safety: catfishing, luring, predators, location tracking, and more. Some related topics are covered elsewhere in this book. The next section is devoted to cyberbullying, for example, and in Chapter 3 you read about reputation management and privacy.

Catfishing happens when someone creates a fake profile and pretends to be someone else. That might be a real person (e.g., someone everyone knows at school) or a fake identity customized to appeal the targeted person. Usually, the catfisher invests a lot of time and thought into developing a detailed backstory for the fake person they are portraying. The risk is that youth will trust this fake person with personal details or share more than they would normally.

6. Cyberbullying

Bullying online is known as cyberbullying. The attack can take many forms, from insults to threats to libel and reputation destruction. Sometimes the bullying behavior is sexual in nature but not always. Online, the bully might send their aggressive remarks via text, photo, audio, or video. Here are some examples of cyberbullying:

- Sending mean-spirited or hurtful email messages.

- Threatening bodily harm in a text message.

- Building a social media account to ridicule or insult someone.

- Sharing private information to embarrass someone.

Many of these activities can be categorized as criminal acts. This might include:

- Slander or libel, saying things that aren't true.

- Harassment; bothering someone to the point that they don't feel safe.
- Extortion; threatening action (e.g. sharing a nude photo) if someone doesn't comply.
- Child pornography, if nude photos or videos are circulated.
- Assault; threats of physical harm and actual physical harm are both assault.
- Fraud; using someone else's (stolen) identity online.

Both the bullies and the victims of bullying need adults' support. There are social consequences and mental health risks for both groups of youth. More than anything, trusted adults — parents, guardians, teachers — need to listen to youth. Take your youth's concerns seriously and don't dismiss what they are telling you. Be alert to what they are saying as well as the subtext. Thoughtful attention might reveal the underlying issue. In many cases, trusted adults will have an ongoing open communication with youth so the details may be confided willingly. But this is not always the case. Many youth will remain silent or, possibly, confide in a close friend. That silence makes it hard for adults to provide support and/or intervene as necessary.

If adults become aware of a cyberbullying issue, they can help report it. However, most youth won't speak up about cyberbullying even with the most trusted adults in their lives. Empower youth to self-report any cyberbullying they experience as well as incidents they witness. Depending on the severity of the incident, youth and/or adults can take one of the following courses of action:

- Leave the online conversation without responding
- Block the phone number to prevent calls/texts.
- Block and report social media accounts of cyberbullies.
- Take screenshots of bullying behavior to record what's happened
- Type the information and submit a hard copy of the details anonymously.
- Talk to a trusted advisor. (Youth talk to adults. Adults talk to school administrators, social workers, police, etc.).
- Report crimes to the authorities via their non-emergency number or website.

There are many resources available online about cyberbullying: what it is, what to do, and how to prevent it. Facebook has published two of the most useful guides, one for parents and the other for educators. You'll find them here:

- www.facebook.com/safety/bullying/parents
- www.facebook.com/safety/bullying/educators

Be sure to introduce youth to the bystander effect when you talk about cyberbullying. When they observe someone being bullied, they shouldn't presume someone else will deal with it. Rather, they should take action — capture a screen shot, tell a trusted adult, or one of the other actions noted above. Youth with strong digital skills won't be bystanders. Instead, empower them to be proactive digital citizens who help fix wrongs like cyberbullying.

7. Legal Obligations

Before this book ends, I hope you'll consider one last major thing. It's important to let kids and teens make mistakes. I advocate for a society where we can let them goof around, make fashion choices, try out makeup looks, and say the wrong thing (and apologize).

That's what growing up is all about. I don't want my son to have to be society's version of "perfect" every day. One of the wonderful things about digital living is that we are all exposed to a wider range of customs, traditions, opportunities, and more. Let's allow them to explore, within moral, ethical, and legal guidelines, and promise not to hold it against them when they go to look for a job, apply to a university, or take on a community position.

However, there are also legal obligations that come with internet use such as denouncing plagiarism in defense of copyright. Reporting nudity, cyberbullying, catfishing, and other behaviors to the authorities. Sending evidence of illegal activities to the police. Avoiding statements that are libel or slander. Not spreading false information. Using 911 only when necessary and never for prank calls. Respecting others' privacy. And so on …

Conclusion

Welcome to the end of the book and the beginning (or continuation) of your work with your youth. Whether you are a parent, guardian, or teacher, you have the opportunity and obligation to inform and support youth as they learn to live a digital life. Whether youth need an introduction to new digital skills or some more advanced information about a specific skill, they need support. Much of that support will come from peers but trusted adults play an important role. Those adults model best behavior, affirm that it's okay to make digital mistakes, and provide resources to help youth get the best out of the internet.

Trusted adults also have a role in overseeing the mental and physical wellness of youth online. Those closest to tweens and teens will be best able to apply and adapt the strategies in this book to the needs of specific youth. There is no one-size-fits-all solution for every digital problem. Digital living is nuanced and variable. It adjusts to the conditions around it and users adapt to its restrictions. What works for one family won't work for another. What works in one classroom will be different from what works in the classroom next door. Overall, our collective goal is to raise the next generation of digital citizens in a way that helps them be productive and healthy both online and offline. And let's not undersell the importance of play and entertainment, too.

The issues of today might change as technologies evolve. Digital youth are growing up to be digital adults and our aim is to give them adaptable skills that will let them thrive in that future. Understanding social skills, study skills, and safety skills will prepare them to live with augmented reality, artificial intelligence, cryptocurrencies, and other technologies. The early versions of these tools and many more are available today and will become more widely available in the years ahead.

To help track progress through the various skills described in this book, use the Digital Life Skills Master Checklist (available on the download kit). You saw this checklist in Chapter 1. It will give you an overview of all the skills and a place to keep track as each skill is introduced and, ultimately, mastered. Work through the skills in any order that makes sense for your situation. Each family will have a unique sequence and teachers will implement digital skills when they are most needed to support the learning environment. Over time, every youth has the potential to master them all.

Digital life skills are woven into the fabric of digital citizenship. Parents', guardians' and teachers' roles are to provide mentorship and support, not requirements and direction. We should focus on practical tips and actionable information, and a learning environment free of judgments and filled with lots of options for every community's unique needs. This should all be offered with an eye on mental wellness so that youth can enjoy the benefits of digital living in a healthy way, today and always.

Download Kit

Please enter the URL you see in the box below into your computer web browser to access and download the kit.

www.self-counsel.com/updates/dlifeskills/19kit.htm

The download kit includes:

- Worksheets for you to use when needed
- Texting and emoji dictionaries
- — And more!

What's That Emoji?

If you choose to review your youth's messages, you'll discover that emojis are part of how they communicate. While a lot of emojis are used innocently, many emojis have an alternate meaning with a sexual connotation. To help you decipher what you're reading, the following table notes some of the most commonly used emojis.

	banana	penis		lips	kissing
	beer glasses	testicles		mailbox	sex
	bird + bee	foreplay, sex		peach	buttocks or vagina
	boxing glove	condom		pickle	penis
	camel	sexual intercourse (humping)		pointing hand	stimulation of female genitalia
	camera with flash	nude photographs (flashing)		pointing + okay	sexual intercourse
	carrot	penis		rain	ejaculation or orgasm
	cat	vagina (pussy)		rocket	orgasm
	cherries	breasts or virginity		strawberry	vagina
	chicken	penis (cock)		surprised face	oral sex on a male
	circus tent	male erection		sweat droplets	ejaculation or orgasm
	cutlery + taco	oral sex of female genitalia		tongue	oral sex on a female
	donut	anus		tulip	vagina
	eggplant (aubergine)	penis		volcano	orgasm
	fist	hand stimulation of a penis (handjob)		waving hand + peach	spanking
	grapes	male testicles		XX face	x-rated or orgasm
				ying yang	sexual position known as 69

©Digital Life Skills for Youth: A Guide for Parents, Guardians, and Educators by Angela Crocker (Self-Counsel Press, 2019).

What's That
Acronym?

A Texting Dictionary

If you choose to review your youth's messages, the following list will help you decipher these commonly used abbreviations. There are thousands more, including cultural variations. To decipher a specific abbreviation, a simple search online should find the translation for you.

#FF	Flashback Friday	GTFO	Get the f*** out	OOTD	Outfit of the day
#MCM	Man crush Monday	GTG	Good to go	OTW	On the way
#TBT	Throwback Thursday	GTG	Got to go	P911	Parent alert
#TT	Transformation Tuesday	GUFN	Grounded until further notice	POS	Parent over shoulder
#WBW	Way back Wednesday			PIR	Parents in room
#WCW	Woman crush Wednesday	H&K	Hugs and kisses	PTFO	Pass the f*** out
10X	Thanks	HBD	Happy birthday	ROFL	Rolling on floor laughing
10Q	Thank you	HML	Hate my life	ROFLMAO	Rolling on the floor laughing my a** off
411	Information	HMU	Hit me up		
420	Marijuana	HNY	Happy New Year	RT	Retweet
511	Too much information	HRU	How are you?	RU	Are you
69	Sexual position	IDC	I don't care	SMH	Shaking my head
AFK	Away from keyboard	IDK	I don't know	SOOF	Swear on our friendship
AMA	Ask me anything	IG	Instagram	STFU	Shut the f*** up
ASL	Age/sex/location	IKR	I know, right	TBH	To be honest
ATM	At the moment	ILY	I love you	TDTM	Talk dirty to me
BF	Boyfriend	IMO	In my opinion	TFTA	Thanks for the add
BFF	Best friend(s) forever	IMU	I miss you	TMB	Tweet me back
BRB	Be right back	J/K	Just kidding	TMI	Too much information
BTW	By the way	KWIM	Know what I mean?	TL;DR	Too long; didn't read
DAFAQ	The f***	L4L	Like for like	TTYL	Talk to you later
DGAF	Don't give a f***	L8R	Later	TXT	Text
DM	Direct message	LMK	Let me know	TYSM	Thank you so much
DTF	Down to f***	LOL	Laughing out loud	TYVM	Thank you very much
F4F	Follow for follow	LMAO	Laughing my a** off	W/E	Whatever
FML	F*** my life	LMFAO	Laughing my f***ing a** off	WDYWFM	What do you want from me?
FOB	Fresh off the boat	MOFO	Motherf***er	WGAFF	Who gives a flying f***?
FTW	For the win.	NBD	No big deal	WKD	Weekend
FWB	Friends with benefits	NM	Nothing much	WTF	What the f***?
FYEO	For your eyes only	NP	No problem	WTGP	Want to go private?
G2G	Got to go	NSFW	Not suitable/safe for work	WYFM	Would you f*** me?
GF	Girlfriend	NVM	Never mind	XOX	Hugs and kisses
GNOC	Get naked on camera	OFC	Of course	YOLO	You only live once

©Digital Life Skills for Youth: A Guide for Parents, Guardians, and Educators by Angela Crocker (Self-Counsel Press, 2019).